MW00344915

THE SEVEN DEADLY SINS

A SURVIVAL GUIDE

REBECCA KONYNDYK DEYOUNG

Unless otherwise indicated, Scripture quotations in this publication are from the Holy Bible, New Revised Standard Version, © 1989, Division of Christian Education of the National Council of the Churches of Christ in the United States of America.

Author Rebecca Konyndyk DeYoung has taught at the college level for over eight years and led church youth group and high school education programs in local churches for more than a decade. Much of that teaching has focused on the seven deadly sins.

The Seven Deadly Sins: A Survival Guide. © 2007, Faith Alive Christian Resources 2850 Kalamazoo Ave. SE, Grand Rapids, MI 49560. All rights reserved. With the exception of brief excerpts for review purposes, no part of this book may be reproduced in any manner whatsoever without written permission from the publisher. Printed in the United States of America on recycled paper.

We welcome your comments. Call us at 1-800-333-8300 or e-mail us at *editors@faithaliveresources.org*.

ISBN 978-1-59255-421-8

10 9 8 7 6 5 4 3 2 1

I would like to acknowledge the students in my Aquinas seminars, whose presentations sparked many ideas for the interactive parts of the curriculum; Calvin College, who gave me a Lilly Faculty Scholars Grant; the Calvin Alumni Association for a grant to edit and further develop the curriculum toward publication, and in particular, my students Nathan Brink and Gretchen Lemmer, who helped me rewrite and edit the curriculum at two crucial stages.

—Rebecca Konyndyk DeYoung

Contents

Introduction

"To flee vice is the beginning of virtue."
—Horace, *Epistles*

The Seven Deadly Sins: Then and Now

"Greed, gluttony, lust, envy, [and] pride are no more than sad efforts to fill the empty place where love belongs, and anger and sloth [are] just two things that may happen when you find that not even all seven of them at their deadliest ever can" (F. Buechner, *Whistling in the Dark*).

Most Christians today have forgotten about this list of seven sins. Either that or they misunderstand the vices on it. Perhaps that is because it is so old—this collection of vices dates back to the earliest centuries of the Christian church. It was originally designed to examine the impact of sin on our own spiritual formation. It was meant to give us a roadmap for self-examination and a plan for spiritual development.

This course is a new study on the seven vices. We wrote it to recapture the wisdom of that ancient tradition and to help contemporary Christians walk with Christ more faithfully in their lives today.

Be Transformed!

We don't often use the language of virtues and vices anymore. But many early Christians used virtue and vice talk to describe the process the apostle Paul talks about in his letter to the Colossians:

> Put to death, therefore, whatever in you is earthly. . . . These are the ways you also once followed, when you were living that life. But now you must get rid of all such things . . . seeing that you have stripped off the old self with its practices and have clothed yourselves with the new self, which is being renewed in knowledge according to the image of its Creator (Col. 3:5, 7-10).

In this passage, Paul tells Christian believers that faith is supposed to change us. To believe is to follow the way of Christ. And to follow means taking off your old, sinful nature, with its habits of thought and behavior, and become someone new. Put on your new identity in Christ, he says, with its renewed and godly habits of thought and behavior. Let the Spirit transform you.

Christian thinkers in the early church and throughout the Middle Ages thought of "taking off the sinful nature" and "putting on Christ" as a transformation of character (Rom. 12:2). They described the sinful nature in terms of vices, and the sanctified nature in terms of virtues—virtues like those listed in Colossians 3:12-14: "Clothe yourselves with compassion, kindness, humility, gentleness and patience. . . . And over all these virtues put on love, which binds them all together in perfect unity" (TNIV). The transformation from a vicious to a virtuous character is a way of describing the process of sanctification. This is the heart of spiritual formation.

How Do the Virtues and Vices Help Us?

This way of thinking about becoming more Christlike in our character helps Christians in two ways.

First, it starts from a real role model, someone who lived out this ideal—Christ himself. The goal is to look at Jesus (Heb. 12:1-2) and strive to be like him.

What does the virtue of Christian courage look like? Watch Jesus when he faced suffering, pain, fear, and death. When we struggle with the vice of greed, we recall Jesus' life of poverty and simplicity, which shows us how to entrust our needs to God rather than building bigger barns to secure the future for ourselves. We learn how the vice of wrath undercuts both gentleness and righteous anger when we see what provokes Jesus: "Smite his cheek, and he turns you the other; slap the dignity of the house of prayer, however, and he turns over a table" (G. Keizer, *The Enigma of Anger*). Christ's example gives us the perfect pattern of virtue. To become like him is to have abundant life and fullness of joy (John 10:10; 15:11).

Second, the virtues and vices take our general goals—"getting rid of the sinful nature" and "being more like Jesus"—and focus them into specific areas of self-examination and spiritual discipline. Before we can get rid of sin, we need a diagnosis. Before we can try to be like Jesus, we need to see how patterns and practices shape a life. How can we be guilty of gluttony even if we don't overeat? How can the discipline of silence help counter our tendencies to vainglory? Put together, the seven vices serve as specific guides to spiritual renewal.

The Tree of Vices

The picture of spiritual *mal*formation that medieval Christians used to represent the seven capital vices is a tree. The sin of pride is the root and trunk that upholds and nourishes the tree. The tree itself has seven main branches. Each of those branches, in turn, has many smaller branches that bear fruit. Everything on the tree is the outgrowth and offspring of its corrupted source, pride.

The idea behind the tree picture is this: If your goal is to get rid of sin in your life, you can't just keep picking fruit off the top branches. More fruit will grow—unless you get the source of the problem. Your aim, therefore, is to chop off the branches that bear the fruit, and ultimately, to take an axe to the trunk of the tree itself.

THE TREE OF VICES

Pride is the root of the vices

Gluttony: Enjoyment of the senses, Uncleanness, Scurrility, Talkativeness, Inappropriate jollity, Inebriation, Drunkenness

Lust: Haste, Love of oneself, Hatred of God, Instability, Petulance, Blindness of mind, Inconsiderateness, Affection for the World, Lack of self-control

Sloth: Wandering mind, Cowardice, Indifference, Not doing good deeds, Error in faith, Sadness, Desperation

Anger: Yelling, Bombast, Blasphemy, Indignation, Assault, Rage, Hatred

Vainglory: Disobedience, Presumption, Discord, Bragging, Singularity, Obstinacy, Hypocrisy

Avarice: Rapine, Theft, Treason, Fraud, Perjury, Usury, Simony

Envy: Resentment of the prosperity of others, Evil Deeds, Pleasure in the suffering of others, Slander, Conniving, Muttering against someone, Homicide

Fruits of the flesh

Way toward death

The Branches

The main branches of the tree of vice are the seven capital vices or deadly sins. Take, for example, the vice of envy. Envy, as one author put it, is "the consuming desire to have everybody else [be] as unsuccessful as you are" (F. Buechner, *Wishful Thinking*). In other words, if the envious can't be the best at something, then they will make sure no one else can either. The underlying desire to be superior, to be "number one," fuels envy's bitterness at others' success and reflects its rootedness in pride. Envy also "branches out" into other vicious traits like spitefulness and rejoicing at the downfall of others. It ultimately bears the "fruit" of hatred—hatred of others for being better and hatred of God for giving others better gifts.

The Wrong Recipe for Happiness

Why is envy such a powerful and prolific evil habit in our lives? Like the other seven, it takes a strong, natural human desire for something good—in this case, the need to be unconditionally accepted and affirmed by others—and twists it into something evil. The envious seek to manufacture value for themselves by putting others down, rather than receiving self-worth as a gift from God. "Wickedness is always easier than virtue, for it takes the shortcut to everything." (S. Johnson, *Boswell: Journey of a Tour to the Hebrides*). Envy's shortcut, however, is doomed to fail. God is the only one who can fulfill us and give us joy. When our pride leads us to take his place and fill this need for ourselves on our own terms, we end up confessing with Saint Augustine,

> My sin was this, that I looked for pleasure, beauty, and truth not in [God] but in myself and in his other creatures, and the search led me instead to pain, confusion, and error (*Confessions*).

We all have deep desires for pleasure, recognition, acceptance, and security. Vices like lust, vainglory, envy, and greed take good human desires for good things and distort them into demonic masters that leave us empty and unfulfilled. Each vice has a relentless, addictive quality, because we are trying to use them "to fill the empty place inside of us that belongs to God alone" (B.B. Taylor, *Home by Another Way*). Each failed attempt at fulfillment leaves us hungrier and more desperate than we were before. When good things are wrongly pursued, sin happens. As sin accumulates, our characters becomes warped and misshapen as well.

The Tree of Virtues

The picture of godly spiritual formation was also a tree—this time a tree of *virtues*. This tree's branches were the qualities of character that make us more like Jesus—virtues like courage, justice, wisdom, and hope. As Jesus says in John's gospel, the mark of a disciple is to "bear much fruit" (John 15:8). Of course, the root of this tree was self-giving love, not selfish pride. Like many early Christians, Saint Augustine understood all the virtues as fruits or forms of love:

> Courage is love readily bearing all things for the sake of God; justice is love serving only God, and therefore ruling well everything else that is subject to the human person; [wisdom] is love discerning well what helps it toward God and what hinders it (Augustine, *On the Morals of the Catholic Church*).

These pictures of vice and virtue lead us to ask ourselves, Where are *we* rooted? What are the main strengths of our character? Are there patterns to our weaknesses? Naming our sins can be the confessional counterpart to counting our blessings. An accurate diagnosis is the first step toward healing. "To flee vice is the beginning of virtue."

The Task of a Lifetime

This study is therefore meant to take us on a spiritual journey into a deeper relationship with Jesus Christ. Our walk with him is an attempt to imitate his actions—but even more, to become the kind of person he is. The journey depends on the relationship, and is intended to enrich and enliven it. The vices are not merely another set of "thou shalt nots" to avoid with self-satisfied, legalistic hearts. Nor can we purge our life of evil practices on our own effort—for that we need the grace given by the Holy Spirit to work in our hearts. But receiving grace is not a passive thing! It gives us a call to action, a gift to use, and a relationship to cultivate. We show our confidence in God's grace when we seek to grow and keep growing spiritually.

A Curriculum on Spiritual Formation

Our aim in this curriculum it to take the tree of vices and to walk contemporary people though this ancient pattern of growth in godliness. We are convinced that what Christian saints and sages of the past have to say about the different ways sin can entangle us is as insightful and relevant today as the day they wrote it.

Our objective is to help people, especially young people, embark on the same lifelong journey of spiritual progress and practice as Christians before them. We hope to help them do so with discernment and purpose. That means our job is to take centuries of theological wisdom and pastoral advice and translate it into language and life lessons that contemporary Christians can understand and apply to themselves. We've designed each session to be interactive and engaging, full of examples and activities for today's growing Christian.

Each session offers
- a warm-up activity to start students thinking about the topic of the session.
- a definition of the vice or sinful habit.
- an exploration of what the vice looks like in contemporary life and in students' lives in particular.
- spiritual disciplines designed to counter the vices in our lives.

We encourage leaders to select activities and sections from each session to suit their particular audience and time frame.

Why use this course? Why study the vices? C.S. Lewis once said,

> We are half-hearted creatures, fooling about with drink and sex and ambition when infinite joy is offered us, like an ignorant child who wants to go on making mud pies in a slum because he cannot imagine what is meant by the offer of a holiday at the sea (C.S. Lewis, "The Weight of Glory," *The Weight of Glory*).

The point of examining our vices is to turn to the sea. To do so, we need to know ourselves—the vices and sins that cling to us and clutch at us—so that we might turn from them to the abundant life and love that only God can give.

Note

In addition to this leader's guide, you'll need a booklet of student handouts for each student.

1

Discipleship Versus Deadly Sins

What do anger, lust, gluttony, avarice, vainglory, envy, and sloth have in common? Each is one of the seven deadly sins, also known as the seven capital vices. And each is rooted in pride, the source of all sin.

We don't often use the language of virtues and vices anymore. But many early Christians used virtue and vice talk to describe the process the apostle Paul calls "taking off the sinful nature" and "putting on Christ" as a transformation of character (Eph. 4:22-24; Col. 3:9-14; Rom. 12:2). Vices are bad, selfish habits—the grooves of the sinful nature. Virtues are good, godly habits of character that come with the Spirit's work in our hearts. God has equipped us with his power so that we may become like him (2 Pet. 1:3-11). Becoming a virtuous person is to become an imitator of Jesus Christ (Eph. 5:1).

This task starts with a role model—Christ himself. The virtues and vices help us focus this general goal —imitating Christ—into specific areas of self-examination and spiritual discipline. Looking at the vices gives us a specific diagnosis of the habits that hinder us and hold us back. The virtues and spiritual disciplines give us practices and patterns that resist vice and transform our character to be more and more like Jesus'.

Session Focus
Virtues and vices and their role in the life of discipleship.

Session Overview

Step 1	Warm-up: Build Your Own Superhero	Students begin identifying qualities they admire by describing superheroes and real-life heroes.	Materials needed: Handout 1: "Superheroes" Pencils or pens Colored pencils, crayons, or markers; optional
Step 2	Imagine Your Funeral	Students reflect on their own lives and characters by imagining their own funerals.	Handout 2: "In Memoriam"
Step 3	Scripture Study	Students explore how Scripture describes the process of moral formation or sanctification.	Bibles Handout 3: "Building a Christlike Character"
Step 4	The Deadly Seven	Students encounter the seven deadly sins as a practical guide to discipleship.	Handout 5: "Seven Deadly Sins" Handout 6: "Seven Virtues" optional Handout 4: "Name That Vice," optional

Step 1. Warm-up: Build Your Own Superhero

Materials: *Handout 1: "Superheroes"; pencils or pens; colored pencils, crayons, or markers, optional*

Name That Hero

Distribute pencils and student handout 1: "Superheroes." Invite volunteers to describe the superheroes listed and briefly describe their super-powers for those who might not know about each superhero.

Have each person share his or her responses to these questions:
- **Who is your favorite superhero?**

- **If I could have one superhero quality, I would choose . . .**

Have students form pairs or trios. Give them instructions along these lines: **Work with your partner(s) to create the ultimate superhero. First, decide on the top five qualities you want your hero to have. These can be qualities that other superheroes have, like the ability to leap tall buildings in a single bound, or unique abilities you think up on your own. When you've decided what your superhero will be like, sketch a rough draft in the space provided on the handout** ("Build Your Own Superhero!") and name him/her! If you wish, provide colored pencils, crayons, or markers.

After about 5 minutes, or when most groups are done, invite students to share their new superheroes. Have fun with it!

Tip

In step 2 of this session, you'll be asking students to share somewhat personal details about themselves and their values. Lighthearted questions like those in step 1 help "warm up" students for deeper sharing later. If you're short on time and have a group that's already comfortable and open with one another, you could skip step 1 and begin the session with step 2.

Name Your Hero

Now ask:
- **Who are your real-life heroes?**

- **Why do you admire those people?**

- **Describe the person you least want to become like (your anti-hero).**

- **Why don't you want to be like that person?**

Make a transition to step 2 by saying something like, **Let's think about the qualities we admire from a little different angle now.**

Step 2. Imagine Your Funeral

Materials: *Handout 2: "In Memoriam"*

My Life Remembered

Have students turn over their handouts to the side titled, "In Memoriam." Give instructions like these: **Imagine that you died today. What would someone who knew you well say at your funeral service? Take about 5 minutes to write that speech in the space indicated on your handout.**

After about 5 minutes, or when most people are finished, invite volunteers to share what they wrote if they feel comfortable. If students are hesitant to volunteer, read your own eulogy to model openness.

Follow up by saying something like this: **Funerals are perhaps one of the only times we sit down and think about who we are. Often we are too busy living to think about who we are becoming or the shape our character is taking.**

My Life as I'd Like It to Be Remembered
Next point students to the second sentence starter on the handout and give instructions like these: **Write down in a short paragraph the way you *wish* the eulogy at your funeral would be. What do you wish people will say about you when you actually do die? What sort of person do you want to have been?**

Again give volunteers the opportunity to share, if they wish. Then point out the following: **If you're like most people, there is a difference between the person you really are right now and the person you hope to become. You may be asking yourself (for the first time, perhaps) how you might get from who you are to who you ought to be. Bridging that gap is just the exercise in character formation that this series is about.**

Character Analysis
Point students to the "Character Analysis" section of the handout and ask them to list three good qualities or character traits they see in themselves—three things they feel are personal strengths.

Go around the group and have each student share one item on his or her list, asking, **What is your best or most positive character trait as a person? Your greatest spiritual strength?**

Then have students write down three negative character traits or areas of weakness they see in themselves.

Go around the group again, acknowledging, **We all have things we need to work on. What is one of your weaknesses or areas of moral failing as a person?** Encourage openness, but do not force anyone to share.

Wrap up this portion of the session with the following comments:
- **We rarely sit down and reflect on the sort of people we are becoming.**

- **This kind of reflection is a spiritual exercise: it gives us a sense of who we are now, helps us identify things we need to work on, and helps us be intentional about the sorts of people we are trying to become.**

- **Deliberate cultivation of character traits is called "formation" (either "moral formation" or "spiritual formation"). Our characters are formed over time, whether we are intentional about it or not.**

As a transition to the next part of the session, ask, **What do you think it would look like to be intentional about the formation of our character?**

Explain that the remaining sessions in this series on the seven deadly sins will help participants—both students and leader—become more intentional about spiritual formation as disciples of Christ.

Step 3. Scripture Study

Materials: *Bibles; handout 3: "Building a Christlike Character"*

Some Basic Terms and Ideas

Distribute Bibles and handout 3: "Building a Christlike Character."

Ask a volunteer to read aloud the section "Goals and Means" on handout 3.

Clarify if needed, then invite another volunteer to read aloud the section on the handout titled "Virtues and Vices."

Allow students to share their ideas about the "thought starter" questions, but don't spend a lot of time on it. Students may cite the Ten Commandments or the Bible as determining what they view as vices or virtues; they may express societal views as having an impact on what we view as "worse" vices. Affirm any appropriate responses, drawing out also the fact that the character of Jesus—our ideal moral role model—shapes our lists of which traits count as virtues and which ones become more important.

Bible Study

Point students to the section on the handout titled "Getting Practical" and read it aloud.

Have students form groups of two and assign each pair one of the first three passages listed. Give them a few minutes to read their passages and discuss the question with their partners, then call the groups back together and share their responses. Make sure the following points come out:

It's fine to have more than one pair work on the same passage. If you have fewer than six students, you can assign each pair two or more passages.

- In these passages, Paul writes about the lifelong practice of identifying and breaking down bad habits and destructive patterns, and cultivating good habits and constructive patterns in their place. The two go together: turning away from vice and turning toward virtue.

- Paul talks about taking off the "old sinful nature" and putting on the "new regenerated nature." This is the work of the Holy Spirit by grace. But grace requires that we live according to the Spirit, not that we just sit around and wait for God to wave a magic wand.

Read 2 Peter 1:3-11 together. Ask:

- **When God gives us grace, that doesn't mean we're all done being made holy. What does God expect us to contribute to the process?**

- **Do you have any ideas of what types of things we should be doing to become sanctified and more like Christ?** Expect and affirm answers like "pray" and "read the Bible." Explain that prayer and Scripture reading are among many spiritual disciplines. Later sessions will give students a range of disciplines to try.

Step 4. The Deadly Seven

Materials: *Handout 5: "Seven Deadly Sins"; handout 6: "Seven Virtues," optional; handout 4: "Name That Vice," optional*

Tip

Handout 4 (on the reverse side of handout 3) is a quiz titled, "Name That Vice." You won't be using that handout immediately.

The Tree of Vices

Begin this step with this explanation: **We have seen that the vices and virtues are a way of thinking about sanctification and the life of discipleship in concrete terms: Which qualities should we be getting rid of, and what do they look like? Which qualities should we be cultivating, and how do we do that?**

The Christian tradition often identified certain virtues and vices as the main ones.

Distribute handout 5: "Seven Deadly Sins" and make the following points:

- **This picture shows seven vices that we know more familiarly as "the seven deadly sins."**

- **These seven vices are singled out not because they are the worst sins, but because they tend to be sources of other sins in our lives.**

- **The tree picture illustrates this: pride is the root or trunk of the tree, and the source of all the branches. The seven vices are the main branches. Their offspring vices are the vices' poison fruit.**

- **It won't do any good to keep picking off the fruit. We need to cut off the main branches and ultimately, uproot the tree.**

Invite volunteers to read aloud the descriptions of the vices/sins.

Tip

Use these optional activities if you have time at the end of your session.

Optional: The Tree of Virtues

Have students turn to handout 6: "Seven Virtues." Highlight the following points:

- **There is a tree of virtues too. Its root is love.**

- **The list of virtues that grows from this tree is meant to cover all aspects of our character—to depict spiritual health and growth in all major areas of our person—from our thoughts to our feelings to our actions toward God, ourselves, and others, that is with our whole self.**

- **The seven principal virtues are Faith, Hope, Love, Practical Wisdom (prudence), Justice, Courage, and Temperance. As the St. Augustine quote reminds us, they are meant to help us love the Lord our God with all our heart, soul, mind, and strength (Deut. 6:5; Matt. 22:37) that is, with our whole self.**

Optional: Identifying the Seven Deadly Sins

Have students turn to handout 4: "Name That Vice," and invite them to see if they can match each of the seven deadly sins and the few virtues (listed on the righthand side of the page) with the appropriate quote. Allow them to use handout 5: "Seven Deadly Sins" to help them.

Answers:
1. Anger
2. Lust
3. Envy
4. Greed
5. Vainglory
6. Pride
7. Gluttony
8. Sloth

Concluding the Session

Conclude the session with this explanation: **In each of the remaining sessions in this course, we will talk about one of the seven deadly sins and its "poison fruits," and how they all grow out of pride.**

Close with prayer.

For the Next Session

Be sure to save your copy of handout 5: "Seven Deadly Sins" to display in session 2.

Pride:
The Root of Vice

In the Christian tradition from Saint Augustine onward, pride was taken to be the origin of all other sin. It was also taken to be the source of all other capital (or source) vices—the root or trunk of the tree of vices. Although we may think of pride as lording it over other *people*, Augustine and others thought of pride as an attempt to take *God*'s place. Pride makes us want to "play God"—to be the one who determines what happiness and goodness is, and to be the one with the power to provide it. In short, pride leads us to resist and deny our dependence on God. By contrast, with the virtue of humility, we gratefully acknowledge our dependence on God.

Session Focus
Pride as the root of the seven deadly sins; the practice of humility as its opposite.

Session Overview

Step 1	Warm-up: Homemade Recipes for Happiness	Students reflect on ways they look for fulfillment.	Materials needed: Handout 7: "Pride: The Root of Vice"; pencils or pens
Step 2	Naming Pride	Students define pride and its role as the "root" of the tree of vices.	Board or newsprint, chalk or marker; handout 7: "Pride: The Root of Vice"; handout 5: "Seven Deadly Sins" from session 1; Bible
Step 3	Recognizing Pride	Students discuss case studies to identify the two-fold pattern of pride in the other vices.	Bibles for optional activity; handout 8: "Slide into Pride"
Step 4	Life Challenge: Overcoming Pride	Students receive examples of humility and some steps to cultivate humility and resist pride in their own lives.	Handout 9: "New Root—New Fruit"; scissors, optional

Step 1. Warm-up: Homemade Recipes for Happiness

Materials: *Handout 7: "Pride: The Root of Vice"; pencils or pens*

Distribute handout 7: "Pride: The Root of Vice," and invite students to read aloud the quotes in the section "Homemade Recipes for Happiness":

"Ninety-nine percent of us are addicted to something, whether it is eating, shopping, blaming, or taking care of other people. The simplest definition of an addiction is anything we use to fill the empty place inside of us that belongs to God alone."
—Barbara Brown Taylor, *Home by Another Way*

"My sin was this, that I looked for pleasure, beauty, and truth not in God but in myself and other creatures, and the search led me instead to pain, confusion, and error."
—Augustine, *Confessions*

"You made us for yourself and our hearts find no peace until they rest in you."
—Augustine, *Confessions*

"We are half-hearted creatures, fooling about with drink and sex and ambition when infinite joy is offered us, like an ignorant child who wants to go on making mud pies in a slum because he cannot imagine what is meant by the offer of a holiday at the sea."
—C.S. Lewis, "The Weight of Glory," *The Weight of Glory*

Ask the following questions:

- **Which of the "addictions" that Barbara Brown Taylor mentions have you observed in our society? What does it look like?**

- **Where do you think people look most often for pleasure, beauty, and truth—that is, things that make them feel fulfilled or happy?**

- **What would you identify as your most likely "addiction"? Jot down your answer or doodle something to represent it in the blank space by the quotations. If you're willing, share it aloud.**

- **Do you agree with Augustine and C.S. Lewis that these "addictions" and other attachments leave us feeling restless and unfulfilled? Why or why not?**

Tip

This series of questions moves from "out there"—what we observe about other people—to "in here"—personal reflections. Unless you have a group that is already very open and willing to share, don't skip the "out there" questions. If you have a large group, you might like to form foursomes for these questions, both to facilitate openness and to allow everyone to respond in a reasonable amount of time.

Step 2. Naming Pride

Materials: *Board or newsprint, chalk or marker; handout 7: "Pride: The Root of Vice"; handout 5: "Seven Deadly Sins" from session 1; Bible*

Defining Pride

Say, **According to ancient Christian tradition, pride is the root of all the "addictions" and sins these quotes talk about. To see how that makes sense, let's try to define *pride*.**

Ask students to call out anything they think of when they think of the word *pride*. Have a volunteer write down all the suggestions on your board or newsprint.

Then say, **Now let's look at a more theological definition of the word *pride* and see how all these ideas about pride fit with that definition.**

Point students to the section "Defining Pride" on handout 7: "Pride: The Root of Vice," and have someone read it aloud.

Take a minute or two to discuss how the students' ideas about pride relate to the theological definition of pride and to clarify any questions students have, but don't spend too long; step 3 will provide practice in working with the definition of pride and its two-fold pattern.

Review: The Tree of Vice

Show students the picture of the Tree of Vice on handout 5: "Seven Deadly Sins" (from session 1).

Briefly review the following points:

- **The seven deadly sins are called "capital vices," which means they are the source from which other sins—the tree's "poison fruit"—often grow.**

- **This metaphor of branches bearing "good fruit" or "bad fruit" comes from John 15:1-8. Invite a volunteer to read John 15:1-8 aloud.**

- **Pride, in turn, is the root of the tree of capital vices, the source of the deadly sins. So all of the others have pride as their root. We'll see how that works as we go along.**

- **Even if you pick the fruit or cut off the branches, the tree will keep growing as long as the root remains.**

- **The point of picturing the vices this way is to show how we must get to the root and pull it out.**

- **With each of the seven deadly sins, we take a good thing (food, sex, money, love, approval) and decide that it—not God—will fulfill us and make us happy if only we can get it for ourselves. In this way, each vice is rooted in pride—that is, in moving control from God to us.**

Step 3. Recognizing Pride

Materials: *Bibles for optional activity "The Many Faces of Pride"; handout 8: "Slide into Pride"*

Optional: The Many Faces of Pride

If you have time, you may wish to explore some Scripture stories to see how pride lies at the root of other sins.

Recount (or look up and read, or have students retell after reading the passages) the following Bible stories:

- **Moses at the burning bush (Exodus 3:1-15; 4:1-17)**

- **David and Bathsheba (2 Samuel 11-12)**

- **The Parable of the Pharisee and the Tax Collector (Luke 18:9-14)**

Ask the following questions:
- **In a word or two, how would you describe the most obvious problem of Moses? Of David? Of the Pharisee?**

Expect answers like "fear" for Moses, "lust" for David, and "pride" for the Pharisee.
- **It's pretty obvious that the Pharisee suffers from pride. In what ways could Moses' fear and David's lust also be expressions of pride?**

Moses' fear could stem from a prideful goal (as described in the two-fold pattern of pride on handout 8): a desire to determine what was best for himself rather than accept what God wanted him to be. "I know you want this from me, God, but it's too scary and I don't want to go out on a limb for you. I prefer my comfortable life just the way it is."

David's lust stems from prideful means: taking for himself what he wanted on his own terms rather than accepting God's will for his life (he should have been out leading his army—see 2 Sam. 11:1) and being satisfied with what God had given him. "I know you appointed me king and gave me power so that I could lead and protect your people, but I'd rather neglect (and even kill!) my people and use my power to bring myself pleasure instead."

Tip

Watch your time as you work through the case studies. Be sure to leave enough time for step 4. If you're running short on time, choose only a few of the case studies to read and discuss.

Summarize by saying something like this:
We often think of pride only in the form of the arrogant, self-satisfied Pharisee who thinks he doesn't need God. But there are many different ways of resisting God's will in our lives—many ways of trying to take or keep control of our own lives to get what *we* want instead of accepting what God wants for us.

Slide into Pride

Have students look at handout 8: "Slide into Pride," and ask volunteers to read aloud the case studies there. After each study, ask the questions printed on the handout:
Prideful goal:
- **What is happiness, according the main character? How does the main character resist or ignore what God wants (God's goal) in order to get what s/he wants (his/her goal)?**

Prideful means:
- **How does the main character try to achieve his/her self-defined picture of happiness?**

Step 4. Life Challenge: Overcoming Pride

Materials: *Handout "New Root—New Fruit"; scissors, optional*

Thoughts on Humility

Distribute handout 9: "*New Root—New Fruit*" and say something like this: **If we work to uproot pride in our lives, we'll need to plant something in its place or weeds will start to fill in the empty spot. The opposite of pride is humility.**

Give these instructions: **Take a few minutes to look over this page. Then be ready to share with the rest of the group something that struck you as interesting, meaningful, or useful.**

Give students about two minutes to skim the handout, then ask them to share what they picked out.

Making Humility a Daily Spiritual Discipline

Encourage students to try one or both of the ideas from the handout for making humility a daily discipline: reflecting on a quote each day and journaling about living out that quote.

If you wish, provide scissors so students can cut out quotations to carry in their pockets throughout the week.

Close with a prayer for the Spirit to uproot pride and help each participant to grow in humility.

3
Envy:
Feeling Bitter When Others Have it Better

Our culture, focused as it is on competition and comparison, leaves people vulnerable to the deadly vice of envy. From the soccer field to the office, envy draws us into a vicious cycle of desire that can never be satisfied and that poisons our relationship of love with others. Envy is a spiritual vice and it requires a spiritual remedy: knowing the depths of God's unconditional love for us.

Session Focus
The role of comparison and of God's unconditional love in diagnosing and countering envy in our lives.

Session Overview

Step 1	Warm-up: M.A.S.H. Game	Students play a game that leads them to experience envy as they measure players' worth comparatively.	Materials needed: Handout 10: "M.A.S.H."; pencils or pens
Step 2	Defining Envy	Students articulate definitions of envy.	Handout 11: "Shades of Green"
Step 3	What Envy Looks Like	Students practice identifying envy using a matching exercise, film clip, or self-survey.	For choice 1: handout 12: "Is It Envy . . . or Something Else?"; choice 2: DVD of *Amadeus*, DVD player and monitor; choice 3: handout 11: "Shades of Green"
Step 4	Life Challenge: Overcoming Envy	Through studying Psalm 73 and encountering specific spiritual practices, students recognize God's unconditional love as the antidote to envy.	Bibles; handout 13: "Seeing Ourselves Through God's Eyes"

Step 1. Warm-up: M.A.S.H. Game
Materials: *Handout 10: "M.A.S.H."; pencils or pens*

Get this session off to a fun start with a game called M.A.S.H. In this game, students will pretend to assign the housing, spouse, number of future children, and type of vehicle the players will have.

To set up the game:

- Recruit two contestants, both of the same gender.

- Enlist the group's help to fill in the blanks on the square on handout 10: "M.A.S.H." Make sure that some options are extreme—for example, 13 children. For vehicle and marriage partner, include a range of options from great to utterly dismal. The heading "M.A.S.H." already represents four options: Mansion, Apartment, Shack, and House, so you don't need to fill in anything on that side of the square.

To play:

- Have each contestant pick a number from 2 to 7.

- Start with contestant 1.

- Count through the lists of items AND the letters M-A-S-H, eliminating the ones that you land on with the chosen number. The last one left in each group is your winner. Keep counting through until you have only one choice in each category left.

- Repeat the process with contestant 2.

Sample M.A.S.H. board:

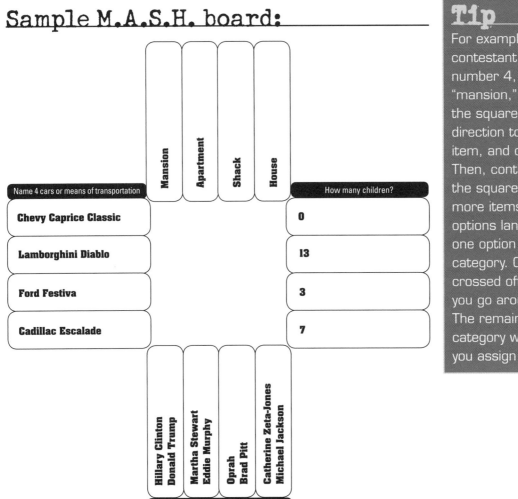

Tip

You'll use just one copy of the student handout for this game—your own—allowing students to play the game on their own copies later—and ideally to recall the lessons of the session.

Tip

For example, if the contestant chooses the number 4, start with "mansion," count around the square in a clockwise direction to the fourth item, and cross it off. Then, continuing around the square, count off four more items, crossing off the options landed on until only one option is left in each category. Once an item is crossed off, don't count it as you go around the square. The remaining option in each category will be the choice you assign to the contestant.

Debrief the game with the following questions and comments:

- **Let's compare the two contestants' futures. Whose life came out better? Worse?**

- To the "losing" contestant: **If you had to change one feature of the "winner's" life, what would it be?** Note that the loser will typically try to inflict maximal damage in a single stroke.

- **The fun of this game depends in large part on comparing ourselves to others, which is fuel for the flames of envy.** Note that envy not only takes the form of wanting to be better (or better off) than someone else, but also delighting in seeing others worse off—in this case, driving a beater, having thirteen kids with an unattractive spouse, and living in a shack.

Step 2. Defining Envy

Materials: *Handout 11: "Shades of Green"*

Definitions

Have students take a look at handout 11: "Shades of Green" (Make sure students don't get distracted by the M.A.S.H. game on the other side of the handout!)

Ask for volunteers to read aloud the definitions on the handout. Then ask, **How would you give a contemporary paraphrase of these definitions? Take a minute to write out your own definition in the space provided.**

When most people have written something, ask students to share their definitions. (For example, someone might define envy as "resenting others for being better than me.")

Growing Like a Weed

Have a volunteer read aloud the section "Growing Like a Weed."

Ask,

- **Can you think of a time when you experienced envy's sharp thorns?** Encourage students to keep that experience in mind as you work through the rest of the session.

- **If, as the quote from Joseph Epstein on the bottom of the handout suggests, "envy is no fun at all," why do we still envy?** Invite responses if students have something to say, but don't belabor the question. It's OK if it simply serves as a thought-provoker.

> **Tip**
>
> If you don't choose the option "Self-Survey" in step 3, you won't be completing the remaining section of this handout ("What's Your Envy Quotient") during the session. Students who are interested can take the handout home and complete the survey on their own.

Make a transition to step 3 by observing that, as miserable as envy makes us, we still find ourselves doing it, as the next part of the session will explore.

Step 3. What Envy Looks Like

Unless your group moves exceptionally quickly, you are unlikely to have enough time to do all of the activities in step 3. Choose the one(s) that will best suit your group.

Choice 1: Matching Exercise

Materials: *Handout 12: "Is It Envy . . . or Something Else?"*

Distribute handout 12 and have students work in pairs to complete the matching exercise. When most pairs are done, go over the correct matches:

1. B
2. E
3. A
4. C
5. F
6. G
7. D

Choice 2: Movie Clip: Amadeus

Materials: *DVD of* Amadeus, *DVD player and monitor*

Before playing the film clip, give the following background information to your students: **The movie opens with the composer Antonio Salieri trying to commit suicide out of guilt for his part in hastening Mozart's death. The two were rivals in 18ᵗʰ-century Vienna. Mozart's talent vastly overshadowed Salieri's, despite Salieri's prayers to God to bless him with musical talent and success. Out of spite, Salieri spends his days trying secretly to destroy Mozart so that he can regain his position of favor as the court composer.**

Show DVD chapter 2 ("Can't name that tune").

Debrief with the following questions and comments:

- **According to the church fathers (leaders in the historical Christian church) like Aquinas, envy destroys our relationships with others and ultimately our relationship with God. How do you see this happen in the film?** Salieri's envy of Mozart and his superior musical talent leads him ultimately to hate Mozart and God, whom Salieri blames for giving him less talent than Mozart. The film's title reflects this: *Amadeus* means "he who is loved by God."

> **Tip**
>
> Motion pictures and videos are fully protected by copyright. However, under the fair use copyright law, teachers in a not-for-profit setting may legally use **brief** excerpts for copyrighted materials in their class sessions. If you are uncertain whether film clips you plan to use are permissible under the "fair use" guideline, either consult a lawyer in your church or apply for a blanket licensing agreement from Christian Video Licensing International (www.cvli.org) for as little as $45 per year.

- **How does the film highlight the competitive nature of envy?** Salieri's self-worth is based on comparing himself to Mozart and finding himself inferior.

- **What does the film suggest about the relationship between envy and self-worth?** Salieri's love for himself is conditional: Only if he is better than his rival can he love and accept himself.

Choice 3: Self-Survey

Materials: *Handout 11: "Shades of Green"*

Say, **All of us struggle with envious thoughts and actions. When these become a *habit*, we have the vice of envy.**

Then lead the discussion with these questions and comments.

- **For what kinds of things do you think people envy others?** Listen to student responses, then point out that things we envy are usually things very important to us—talents and values that are central to our identity and worth as a person.

- **Why do we envy others?** Help students see that envy, at its worst, strikes at the heart of our identity and worth. We envy others who are better than we are in areas central to how we see ourselves. Envy can make us hate ourselves when we don't measure up against others in these areas.

- **Silently reflect on what you personally envy others for. If you're willing, share your responses.**

Point students to the survey "What's Your Envy Quotient?" on handout 11: "Shades of Green." Give them a few minutes to complete the survey and the questions at the bottom. Assure them that they will not have to share any of their responses unless they wish to.

When most people are finished, invite volunteers to share something they learned or any reactions to the survey and the questions.

Step 4. Life Challenge: Overcoming Envy

Materials: *Bibles; handout 13: "Seeing Ourselves Through God's Eyes"*

Scripture Study: Psalm 73

Distribute Bibles and have students turn to Psalm 73. Invite volunteers to read aloud while the rest of the group follows along.

Discuss the psalm with questions such as these:

- **How does the psalm writer describe his own envy?** The writer admits his struggle with envy and almost turns his back on God. He compares his envious state to losing his footing (v. 2), being as ignorant as an animal (v. 22), and feeling as if he is being punished (v. 14).

- **Does he blame God for his problem?** If he doesn't directly blame God as the cause of his troubles, he certainly suggests that God didn't do anything to help him out (vv. 13-14).

- **Where in the psalm do you think he turns a corner toward overcoming his envy?** See verse 17.

- **How would you describe the cure for his envy?** He finds the ultimate cure for envy by seeing himself in God's eyes, rather than by comparing himself with the wicked (vv. 23-26). He learns to defeat envy when he takes the focus off what he and his rivals have done and instead focuses on the goodness of God (v. 28).

Seeing Through God's Eyes

Draw students' attention to handout 13: "Seeing Through God's Eyes."

Read aloud or invite a volunteer to read aloud the passage by Robert C. Roberts.

Ask:

- **What do you think self-confidence and self-worth have to do with envy?** Ultimately, envy is a spiritual self-worth problem and therefore requires a spiritual solution. In this quote, Roberts explains that it is crucial for the envier to stop comparing herself to others and start valuing herself as God does—with *unconditional* love.

- **How aware are you of God's unconditional love for you?**

Daily Practice

Have volunteers read aloud the section "Daily Practice" on the handout. Challenge each student to commit to trying one practice for the next one or two weeks.

Close with prayer for eyes to see God's unconditional love and the discipline to overcome envy.

Tip

For the sake of accountability, have each person say which practice s/he is going to try. On your own copy of the handout, jot each person's name beside the chosen practice so that you can follow up with the students next week.

Sloth:
Lazy About Love

Even more than the other vices, sloth is commonly misunderstood. Originally, sloth was counted as one of the most spiritually dangerous of the seven deadly sins. Today, most people, even Christians, associate sloth with mere laziness. Even busy, hard-working, and active people, however, can find themselves entrapped by sloth without ever recognizing the true source of their inner restlessness.

Sloth is opposed to the effort required to really love another—especially God. The slothful person wants to stay in the easy comfort of a selfish life, instead of heeding God's call to be transformed by love into true Christlikeness.

There are many ways to distract ourselves and deny the demands of God's love on us. The slothful person uses them to ignore the demands of love and to make herself "comfortably numb."

Session Focus
How both busyness and apathy can be symptoms of sloth's resistance to the transforming power of God's love.

Session Overview

Step 1	Warm-Up: Couch Potato Contest	Students play a game that demonstrates how contemporary perceptions of sloth miss the mark.	Materials needed: Set of four crayons for each student: blue, green, orange, and red; handout 14: "Where Does the Time Go?"; baked (or raw) potato in a fancy bag
Step 2	Defining Sloth	Students articulate definitions of sloth.	Handout 15: "Sloth: Being Lazy About Love"; pencils or pens
Step 3	What Sloth Looks Like	Students identify contemporary expressions of sloth in clips from the movie *Groundhog Day* and examine their own lives for symptoms of sloth.	DVD of *Groundhog Day*; DVD player and monitor; handout 16: "Symptoms of Sloth"
Step 4	Life Challenge: Overcoming Sloth	Through studying Scripture passages and encountering specific spiritual practices, students identify ways to overcome the sin of sloth in their lives.	Bibles; handout 17: "Dressed for Discipleship—A Graphic Novel"; handout 18 "Daily Practice"

Step 1. Warm-up: Couch Potato Contest

Materials: *Set of four crayons for each student: blue, green, orange, and red; handout 14: "Where Does the Time Go?"; baked (or raw) potato in a fancy bag*

Optional: Weekly Check-in

If you wish, have students tell about their successes and challenges in doing the daily practices they committed to last week. Be sure to share your own experiences as well. If you prefer, you can do this "weekly check-in" at the end of the session.

> **Tip**
>
> Wendy's® makes cheap, delicious baked potatoes.

Couch Potato Contest

Distribute handout 14: "Where Does the Time Go?" and a set of four crayons (blue, green, orange, red) to each student.

Give instructions like these: **Your timesheet represents one twelve-hour period of a day. The clock graphic represents a typical weekday from 9 a.m. to 9 p.m. Color in segments of the day according to what you usually do that time of day.**

- **Blue: school, study, and work time**

- **Green: basic needs (eating, sleeping, and so on)**

- **Orange: social and recreational time**

- **Red: devotional/"God" time**

For example, if a student is in class from 9 a.m. to 12:30 p.m., she would color that segment with the "school/study work" color (blue). Lunch break from 12:30-1 p.m. would be green; an after-school Bible study from 3:30-4:00 would be red.

Give the students 3-4 minutes to fill out their timesheets. Feel free to complete your own chart too.

> **Tip**
>
> You can vary the colors according to what crayons you have available, but it's easiest if all the students use the same four colors—that way they can tell at a glance what each segment represents. It may be helpful to have one chart colored in to use as an explanatory guide.

Have everyone hold up his or her sheet for the group to see.
Explain that the group will vote on whose diagram reveals him or her to be the most slothful person. The winner will receive a prize.

Ask: **Whose chart shows him or her to be the most slothful person? Why do you think so?**
Go around the group and ask each student to explain his/her vote. Expect them to express some confusion over what sloth is supposed to be.

Give the winner the prize—a baked potato for being the best "couch potato."

Then ask:

- **What colors/categories did you count as the most slothful activities?** Answers usually identify slothfulness with sleeping or doing other activities that students associate with "wasting" time.

- **The least slothful?**

- **Why is that?** Expect answers to reflect the view that sloth is doing nothing, or nothing "worthwhile."

- **Is there anything that makes a Christian's view of sloth different than a non-Christian's?**
  Expect puzzlement in response to this question. Some students may say that sloth for Christians is being lazy about going to church or doing devotions.

Make a transition to step 2 with a comment along these lines: **Most people today misunderstand the deadly sin of sloth. They think sloth is physical laziness, but sloth is really a spiritual vice. It is about being apathetic (not caring) about godliness—so much so that we are unwilling to be changed by God.**

Step 2. Defining Sloth

Materials: *Handout 15: "Sloth: Being Lazy About Love"; pencils or pens*

Distribute pencils or pens and have students turn to handout 15: "Sloth: Being Lazy About Love."

Invite volunteers to read aloud the various quotes on the handout, then give students a few minutes to work independently and write their own definitions of sloth in the space with the sentence-starter, "Sloth is . . ."

When most people are done, have students share their definitions. Definitions should contain the idea that **sloth is resistance to the demands that relationships of love make on us.**

Step 3. What Sloth Looks Like

Materials: *DVD Groundhog Day; DVD player and monitor; handout 16: "Symptoms of Sloth"*

Film Clips: Groundhog Day
In this part of the lesson, you'll use clips from the movie *Groundhog Day* to show how slothful people resist the effort required by relationships of love.

Clip 1: DVD chapter 17
Introduce the first clip with comments like these:
- **In the film *Groundhog Day*, the main character Phil Connors (played by Bill Murray) gets stuck in the small town of Punxatawny, Pennsylvania, inexplicably reliving the same day— Groundhog Day—over and over again.**

- **Smug, self-centered Phil takes advantage of his predicament by setting up an elaborate deception to seduce his producer, Rita (Andie MacDowell).**

- **He does not really love her—at least, not yet. Rather than change himself, he figures out what she wants, and then plays the part, putting up just the right false front—quoting a line of French poetry he memorized overnight, pretending to share her interest in world peace and her taste in ice cream—all the while manipulating her into giving him what he wants (sex).**

- But his cynical and cunning scheme—to use each day to find out more about Rita in order to orchestrate the "perfect date" in which he ultimately gets her into bed with him—betrays his own selfish aims and closes off any possibility for real love between them. Let's watch Phil pursue "love" in his old selfish ways.

Show DVD chapter 17 ("Perfect Guy") after the first snowball fight, when Phil and Rita are walking arm in arm. Start at Rita's line: "I'm just amazed" and play through her line, "That's for making me care about you!" and the next moment of Phil's lonely waking the next day.

Briefly discuss the clip with the following questions:
- **How would you describe Phil's ideas of "love"?** Phil's idea of "love" is based only on fulfilling his own selfish desires. Phil fails to make any genuine effort to love Rita; instead, he pursues the easiest and fastest route to his own gratification, which involves manipulating her instead of changing himself.

- **In what ways is Phil's behavior a good example of sloth? Find some lines on the handout about sloth that describe Phil or his behavior.** Examples could include the following:

    "The slothful person wants to be loved without having to let love transform her."

    "The slothful person *does* want what comes easy, and resists effort—the effort it takes to truly love another person."

    "Love requires selfless giving"—yet all of Phil's "giving" is purely selfish, motivated by his desire to get Rita into bed.

- **Phil isn't lazy in this clip. How do you reconcile that with the idea of sloth?** The measure of sloth is not whether we are busy or lazy, but whether we want everything our way—the way that is easy or comfortable for us—or whether we are willing to give ourselves in love for others. Phil puts a lot of effort into trying to get Rita to give him what he wants without having to give anything back. Phil shows us that the slothful person's unwillingness to accept the demands of real love can take the form of busy activity.

- **Why might a slothful person find it easier to obey a command to work hard than "the greatest commandment" Jesus gives in Matthew 22:37: "Love the Lord your God with all your heart, and with all your soul, and with all your mind"?** Many people think that hard work is the opposite of sloth. But what sloth is really opposed to is not hard work itself, but love.

- **What are the results of Phil's "slothful" pursuit of "love"?** Although she is initially taken in by his schemes, in the end Rita sees through Phil's selfish strategy and rejects his advances. "I can't believe I fell for this!" she cries at him in anger. "You don't love me! You could never love anyone but yourself!" That route leads him to alienation from Rita, rather than a relationship.

Clip 2: DVD chapter 18

Introduce the second clip with comments like these:
- **In the first clip, Phil put a lot of effort into trying to get Rita to give him what he wanted without having to give anything back. We saw that the slothful person's unwillingness to accept the demands of real love can take the form of busy activity.**

- **But sloth can also show up in a more familiar form—apathy, inactivity, and despair. In this next scene, Phil is in despair, and he tries to commit suicide. He can't get what he wants from Rita the way he is, but he also refuses to change. So he is at an impasse.**

Show DVD chapter 18 ("Gobbler's Knob") from the scene of the clock turning slowly from 5:59 to 6:00 a.m. through the *Jeopardy* scene, up to Phil's line "for the rest of your life."

Briefly discuss the clip with the following questions:

- **Why do you think Phil tries to commit suicide?** Phil cannot endure a life completely devoid of real love, but is also unwilling to become the sort of person who can really love others. In this way, sloth can lead to despair.

- **In what ways does Phil's relationship with Rita parallel human relationships with God?** We can be happy only in a relationship of genuine love for God. When we refuse the demands for selfless giving that a relationship requires, we are left alone, loveless, and unfulfilled.

Clips 3 and 4: DVD chapters 25 and 27

Introduce two final clips with comments like these:

- **In the rest of the movie, Phil finally tries a new tactic: to take off his old, selfish self and— step by step—genuinely become a better person, one who learns to live for others and love them, not just himself.**

- **In this scene we see that Phil's transformation of character requires abandoning his old, self-gratifying ways. This takes effort on his part—as much as pursuing his previous selfish schemes. Only with his change of heart, however, can he finally find love and meaning in life —a change that shows him how real happiness comes from giving himself in love to others.**

Play DVD chapter 25 ("Rock-maninoff") where Phil and Rita are dancing at the town party, up to Phil's line "Do you want the long or the short version?"

Next play DVD chapter 27 ("A Warm Face") up to Rita's line "I think I'm happy too."

Briefly discuss the clips with the following questions:

- **How would you describe Phil's view of love now?** Phil is happy making Rita happy—without getting her into bed *or* getting out of Groundhog Day. Only learning to love selflessly ends the curse to repeat Groundhog Day over and over again and wins him Rita's love in return.

- **Compare the "new Phil" to the despairing Phil we saw in the second clip. What's different?** Unlike his old self, the new Phil is no longer bored and restless, filling time with self-centered diversions and empty pleasures. This time he does not merely pretend to be but really becomes not just a poet and pianist, but a person capable of unselfish love.

- **What would you say Phil's motivations are now?** Phil is no longer motivated by the sole desire to get what he wants in his relationship with Rita. Instead, his help for others shows that he has learned to genuinely care about others—for their own sake.

- **Contrast the busyness we saw in Phil at the beginning with the way Phil is now. What can that teach us about busyness in relationship to sloth?** We can see through Phil's example that the slothful person can be very busy and active—that is, very busy trying to get what *he* wants *without* having to change himself. In contrast, true love transforms us. The real work here is not just physical effort, but a change of heart.

Optional: Digging Deeper

If you have time, you may also wish to explore how *Groundhog Day* illustrates sloth's two main expressions: *apathy* and *active avoidance*.

Share the following points, inviting students to identify ways the movie illustrates them and to suggest contemporary applications in real life.

When we apply sloth to our relationships to God, it can look like this:
The apathy vice:
- **Its original name, *acedia* (pronounced ah-kay-dia) means "not caring" (*a* = not, *kedeia* = care) or apathy.**

- **When I am slothful in this way, I couldn't care less about my own spiritual state, the needs of others, or what God wants me to become.**

- **Instead of seeking to grow in love, I choose a self-serving, complacent, and comfortable life.**

- **God has called us to live for him and to dedicate our lives to loving God and others. When sloth has its grip on us, we give up on this identity and purpose. Boredom, resignation, and despair set in.**

- **Like Phil in the "Jeopardy" clip (2), this form of sloth is expressed through laziness or apathy.**

The avoidance vice:
- **Sloth can also wear the mask of busyness—when our activity is a cover-up for avoiding God and acknowledging what he calls us to become.**

- **When I am slothful in this way, I seek activities that help me escape facing those demands or distractions that help me deny them.**

- **One of the best coping strategies for the slothful person is to stay busy—with work, recreation, or even church activities—too busy, that is, to think about what she is doing and why.**

- **If we don't allow ourselves to rest, then we won't have to acknowledge that our restless activity is a distraction or cover-up for our lack of acceptance of what God really wants from us.**

- **Like the old Phil (clip 1), whether our activities are work-related or recreational, this form of sloth is expressed through busy activity.**

Symptoms of Sloth

Direct students' attention to handout 16: "Symptoms of Sloth," and have a volunteer read aloud the top section, stopping at the self-survey.

Ask:
- **Which of these behaviors are difficult to recognize as sloth in our own lives?**

- **Which are the easiest?**

- **What examples can you give of these behaviors from real life—maybe even your own life?**

> **Tip**
>
> You may want to play R.E.M.'s "It's the End of the World as We Know It" (". . . and I feel fine"—a tongue-in-cheek illustration of the apathy of sloth) and/or Pink Floyd's "Comfortably Numb" (about escapism through drugs) while students are filling out their Sloth Self-Surveys.

Next, give students a few minutes to complete the "Sloth Self-Survey" on the handout.

When students are done with the self-survey, make a transition to the next step by saying something along these lines: **If we know we're slothful, is there anything we can do about it? Let's end the lesson talking about practices for shaking off sloth.**

Step 4. Life Challenge:
Overcoming Sloth

Materials: *Bibles; handout 17: "Dressed for Discipleship—A Graphic Novel; handout 18: "Daily Practice"*

Dressed for Discipleship

Have students turn to handout 17: "Dressed for Discipleship—A Graphic Novel" and work independently or in pairs to complete the graphic novel with dialogue, narration, and illustrations where needed. Hand out Bibles and encourage students to put the message of the Bible passages in their own words.

When most students are done, read the handout aloud, stopping at each blank to allow students to share what they drew and wrote.

After you've read the entire handout and everyone has had a chance to contribute, ask:

- **How do the messages from Paul and Peter help you understand the sin of sloth?**

- **What practical application can you draw for your own life? Be specific.**

Daily Practice: Living the Transformation

Distribute handout 18: "Daily Practice" and have volunteers read it aloud. Challenge each student to commit to trying one practice for the next one or two weeks.

Close with prayer for the power to choose love over sloth.

Tip

For a very effective visual aid, wear frumpy old clothes for the majority of the session, then, during this section, take off the old clothes and put on sharp-looking clothes. Make sure you have adequate and modest clothing on underneath the articles you are taking off and putting on!

Tip

For the sake of accountability, have each person say which practice s/he is going to try. On your own copy of the handout, jot each person's name beside the chosen practice so that you can follow up with them next week.

5

Avarice:
I Want It ALL

Most people know the vice of avarice by its modern name, greed. Greed is very familiar to us—we see it displayed on TV commercials, movies, and popular music, and evidenced in our own purchases of clothes, electronics, cars, and toys. This session examines the vice of avarice in light of a Christian perspective on money and possessions.

Session Focus
Generosity and trust as antidotes to avarice.

Session Overview

Step 1	Warm-up: "Feed Your Greed" Game	Students play a game that tests the limits of what they would do for money.	Materials needed: Two glasses of water; five food products that can mixed in water; a spoon; $3 in an envelope labeled "Prize money"
Step 2	Defining Avarice	Students articulate definitions of avarice.	Handout 19: "Avarice: Wanting It All"; pencils or pens
Step 3	What Avarice Looks Like	Students apply the categories of avarice, liberality, and prodigality to biblical and contemporary examples and assess their own use or misuse of possessions.	For choice 1: handout 20: "The Golden Mean"; choice 2: handout 21: "Got Greed?"; three chairs; Bibles; three signs: *Stinginess, Liberality, Prodigality*; props, optional
Step 4	Life Challenge: Overcoming Avarice	Through studying Scripture passages and encountering specific spiritual practices, students identify ways to overcome the sin of avarice in their lives.	Bibles; handout 22 "In God We Trust"; handout 23: "Daily Practice"

Step 1. Warm-up: Feed Your Greed Game
Materials: *Two glasses of water; five food products that can be mixed in water; a spoon; $3 in an envelope labeled "Prize money"*

If you wish, have students tell about their successes and challenges in doing the daily practices they committed to last week. Be sure to share your own experiences as well. If you prefer, you can do this "weekly check-in" at the end of the session.

"Feed Your Greed" Game

Hold up the envelope of money labeled "Prize money." Say:

- **I have a cash prize for the person who accepts the most extreme challenge in this game.**

- **Would any of you accept the challenge of drinking this glass of water for the cash prize? Expect almost all hands to go up. I will continue to add ingredients to the glass until only one person will accept the challenge.**

> **Tip**
> Some good food products to mix in the water are chocolate syrup, grape jelly, ketchup, salad dressing, salsa, and refried beans.

One by one (working from most to least appetizing) add ingredients to the water. After each ingredient is added, ask, **Is anyone still willing to drink all of this mixture for the prize money?**

When only one person is left, have him or her drink the concoction. Hand over the prize money. (It would be considerate to have a glass of plain water for the winner to drink after the concoction.)

Debrief the game with comments and questions like these:

- **What shows are on TV right now that get people to do outrageous or unpleasant things for money?**

- **What makes people want to be on these shows? What makes people want to watch them?**

- **Games like that prey on people's greed—or avarice as it's called in the list of seven deadly sins. What other examples have you seen of appealing to people's avarice or greed? Students may suggest advertising, various forms of media, or social pressures.**

> **Tip**
> If you still have several volunteers after you've stirred in all your additives, pour the liquid into several glasses and let each one drink it. Have them share the prize money.

Step 2. Defining Avarice

Materials: *Handout 19: "Avarice: Wanting It All"; pencils or pens*

Distribute pencils or pens and handout 19: "Avarice: Wanting It All."

Invite volunteers to read aloud the various segments on the handout, then give students a few minutes to work independently and write their own definitions of avarice in the space after the sentence starter "Avarice is . . .".

When most people are done, have students share their definitions. Help students realize that definitions should contain the idea that greed/avarice is primarily a heart problem—a problem with what we love most. If we love God and people most, then we will use money and possessions for their sake, as is appropriate. However, if we love money and possessions too much, we will try to use other people and even God for our own gain. This disorder of the heart is avarice.

Step 3. What Avarice Looks Like

You won't have time to do all the activities and options suggested for step 3. Choose those that best fit the needs of your group.

Choice 1: The Golden Mean

Materials: *Handout 20: "The Golden Mean"; three chairs; Bibles; three signs:* Avarice, Liberality, Prodigality; *props, optional*

Have students turn to handout 20: "The Golden Mean," and have volunteers read aloud the definitions of avarice/stinginess, liberality/generosity, and prodigality/wastefulness along the continuum.

Set out three chairs and attach three signs (*Avarice, Liberality,* and *Prodigality*) to the chairs. Explain the activity as follows: **We will consider four stories or passages and try to identify each one as a case of avarice, liberality, or prodigality according to the attitude about money it exemplifies. We'll need a volunteer for each story who will sit in the appropriate chair as directed by the rest of the group.**

Recruit a volunteer for Case 1. Have the volunteer read the Scripture text for Case 1 (see handout for scripture references). Ask the group to decide which category the case illustrates, and have the volunteer sit in the correct chair and hold the designated sign. Discuss the question from the handout after Case 1, and then repeat the process with the other cases.

Guide students to identify the illustrations as follows:
Case 1 (Luke 21:1-4 and Matthew 27:57-60): **Liberality**

- The key to liberality is not the quantity given away in and of itself (two copper coins or a new tomb), but the this reveals the heart of the copper giver and his or her attachment to money.

Case 2 (Luke 15:11-32): **Prodigality**

- Freedom and generosity clearly do not mean that we should not value money or be wise in saving or using it. It is not good to spend more than we earn and give unwisely. In fact, doing so is also a vice—known as prodigality. It's this vice that the prodigal son was guilty of. The prodigal's foolish waste of money is a double error: he spent too much, and spent it on things he should not have spent money on.

Case 3 (Genesis 13:1-13): **Avarice**

- When your love of money is in proper alignment with your love of God, you won't grab more than your share or hoard up all the good stuff for yourself. Lot gives us an example of selfish acquisition and overvaluing possessions—taking the best or most for yourself with no thought for others. Later on, Lot's wife was so attached to her home that the angels had to drag her out of the city and still she turned back in longing at what she'd left behind.

> **Tip**
>
> For extra visual reinforcement, give a prop to each volunteer who sits in the chair:
> - Case 1: two small copper coins
> - Case 2: Daddy's credit card
> - Case 3: sign that says: I want the biggest and the best
> - Case 4: letter paper and pen

> **Tip**
>
> Form two teams and let each team come up with its own stories to illustrate the three perspectives on money. Have each team present its stories and have the other team identify the perspectives they illustrate.

- Notice that in this story their greed affected their whole family and placed many people in a situation of spiritual and physical danger. Lot landed in the city of Sodom as a result of his choice, with dire consequences later for him and his whole family. Greed is not just a private or internal sin.

Case 4 (Philippians 4:1-14, 18-19): **Liberality**

- The virtue of liberality gives us freedom from needing to possess things for ourselves—whether a lot or a little.

Choice 2: Avarice Infection: Diagnosing the Problem

Materials: *Handout 21: "Got Greed?"*

Direct students' attention to handout 21: "Got Greed?" Give students a few minutes to work independently to complete the self-survey on the handout.

When most people are done, use the following questions and comments to guide students to think further about the areas in which they personally struggle with the sin of avarice:

- **Taking a vow of voluntary poverty is a traditional way of imitating Christ. Imagine that you've decided to simplify your lifestyle so that you have only what you really need—two sets of clothes, for instance, a bus pass instead of a car, and so on. On a scale of 1 (easy) to 10 (really hard), how hard do you think it would be to give up your nonessentials?**

- **What would be the hardest thing to give up: clothes, music, electronics, junk food, or something else?**

- **Are Christians different than the rest of society in terms of how much we own? Do you think Christians should be different? Explain.**

- **Is having lots of money a bad thing? Be clear that money itself is not either good or bad— it's how we use it and how much we are attached to it that is the problem.**

- **On the positive side, what is the best example of generosity that you have either experienced or witnessed? What motivated that generosity?**

Read aloud the quote from the bottom of the handout: **"It is enough for us to have only a little, so we should in general give away more than we keep." —Thomas Aquinas**

Ask:
- **Do you agree or disagree with Thomas Aquinas on this? Why?**

- **What percentage of what you earn do you give away?**

Optional: Greed—It's a Justice Issue!

Use this optional activity to help students see that acquiring and keeping money or stuff can become so important to us that we are willing to deprive others of it in order to get what we want.

Read aloud the following quote from Saint Ambrose, a great moral teacher:
   It is the hungry one's bread that you hoard,

the naked one's cloak that you retain,
the needy one's money that you withhold.
Wherefore as many as you have wronged you might have aided.

Suggest that a contemporary paraphrase might read like this:

The food spoiling in the back of your overstocked refrigerator belongs to the child who came to school yesterday with no breakfast, the new winter coat hanging in your closet next to four others (now out of style) belongs to the homeless person you passed on your way downtown last weekend, and the savings you stockpile for retirement is the difference between subsistence and starvation for the sweatshop workers who made your favorite golf shoes. Wherefore as many as you have wronged you might have aided.

Provide paper and pencils or pens and challenge students to write examples that relate to their own possessions and experiences. You may want to write the following pattern on your board or newsprint as an example: **The** _____ **[something you have] belongs to** _____ _____ **[someone in need of it].**

After everyone has had time to write at least a few examples, have students read their examples to the rest of the group.

If time permits, recount briefly the story of Achan's sin found in Joshua 7.

Ask: **Who *is* the rightful owner of the stuff we have?**

Optional: Why Is It So Easy to Hoard?

Aquinas mentions two natural hindrances to giving money and material goods away: earning it yourself and a past experience of poverty.

1. Earning it yourself
Share the following story with your students:

As we were growing up, my brother and I would always fight over who got to put the money in the collection plate in Sunday mornings. We thought it was fun and a privilege. But when I started earning my own money babysitting and mowing lawns, it was much harder and less fun to take a dollar out of a meager afternoon's earnings, and give it away in that same offering plate.

Ask: **Whose money do you find easier and more fun to spend or give away—yours or others'? Explain.**

2. A past experience of poverty
Share the following story with your students:

My grandfather grew up during the Great Depression in the early twentieth century. During many cold Michigan winters he did without hot water in order to have enough money to live on. Even when he was old and had become comfortably wealthy, when he took his grandson out to a restaurant for dinner, he would eat his meal at the nursing home first to avoid spending money at the restaurant on his own dinner too.

Sometimes the desire for financial security becomes a form of avarice that keeps people from spending money on even worthwhile things.

Ask: **Do you ever take more pleasure in acquiring and keeping money (or possessions) than on spending it (or using them)? Can you think of story of your own that illustrates this?**

Offer this challenge from one of the Church Fathers:
> **"God gives some excess riches so that they might have the merit of good stewardship."**
>
> —Thomas Aquinas

Tip

For the sake of accountability, have each person say which practice s/he is going to try. On your own copy of the handout, jot each person's name beside the chosen practice so that you can follow up with them next week.

Discuss the following questions:
- **Why do you think God has given you what you have?**
- **What does God intend you to do with it and use it for?**

Step 4. Life Challenge: Overcoming Avarice

Materials: *Bibles; handout 22: "In God We Trust"; handout 23: "Daily Practice"*

In God We Trust
Form groups of no more than three and assign each group one of the passages on handout 22: "In God We Trust." (If you have more than three groups, it's OK to assign the same passage to more than one group.)

Give the groups about five minutes to read their passages and respond to the thought-starters, then gather everyone together again. Have each group summarize its passage and share the responses.

As you have time, invite volunteers to describe times when they have experienced the freedom from avarice that trusting God can bring.

Daily Practice
Distribute the student handout "Daily Practice" and have volunteers read it aloud. Challenge each student to commit to trying one practice for the next one or two weeks.

Close with prayer for freedom from avarice and the grace to trust God more fully.

6

Vainglory:
Image Is Everything

"Vainglory" is not a familiar term in contemporary society, although people still recognize its close cousin, "vanity." In lists of the seven deadly sins, people often confuse and conflate vainglory and pride. Though vainglory is closely connected with pride, vainglory is not so much the elevation of one's *self*, but of one's *image* in the eyes of others. If pride is after position, vainglory is after popularity. The vainglorious person attempts to win recognition and approval from others in a disordered way, and our image-obsessed culture only encourages us to make this vice our life's focus.

Session Focus
Giving glory to God, not to oneself.

Session Overview

Step 1	Warm-up: Distorted Reality TV	Skits or talk about celebrities introduce the concept of vainglory.	Materials needed: Paper and pencils if you choose the alternate warm-up activity
Step 2	Defining Vainglory	Students define vainglory and categorize examples of vainglory according to its four basic forms.	Handout 24: "Vainglory: Image Is Everything"; pencils or pens
Step 3	What Vainglory Looks Like	Students identify contemporary expressions of vainglory in the movie *Beauty and the Beast* and examine their own lives for symptoms of vainglory.	DVD of Walt Disney's *Beauty and the Beast*; DVD player and monitor; handout 25: "Christians in the Limelight"; handout 26: "Vainglory Self-Survey"; CD with song "Legacy" by Nichole Nordeman and CD player, optional
Step 4	Life Challenge: Overcoming Vainglory	Through studying Scripture passages and encountering specific spiritual practices, students identify ways to overcome the sin of vainglory in their lives.	Bibles; handout 27: "Good Glory!"; handout 28: "Vanquishing Vainglory: Simple Steps and Going Further"; copies of *Celebration of Discipline* by Richard Foster, optional

Step 1. Warm-up: Distorted Reality TV

Materials: *Paper and pencils if you choose the alternate warm-up activity*

Optional: Weekly Check-in

If you wish, have students tell about their successes and challenges in doing the daily practices they committed to last week. Be sure to share your own experiences as well. If you prefer, you can do this "weekly check-in" at the end of the session.

Distorted Reality TV

Form groups of three to four students and give these instructions: **Each group has about five minutes to prepare to act out a reality TV show, commercial, or infomercial that shows how TV encourages people to improve their *image*.**

Assign each group a show from the suggestions below, have them choose from the list, or have them come up with their own ideas.

- **Home remodeling show:** *Trading Spaces*

- **Makeover show:** *Swan, Extreme Makeover*

- **Workout equipment infomercial:** *Bowflex, Total Gym*

- **Car refurbishing show:** *Pimp My Ride*

- **Fashion and style:** *E!*

- **Plastic surgery show:** *Dr. 90210*

- **Commercials:** *Rogaine Hair Growth, Maybelline Mascara, Gap Clothing, Diet Solutions*

> ### Tip
> For extra fun, supply props or costumes for groups to use in presenting their skits.

After about five minutes, have the groups perform their skits. Debrief with questions like these:

- **In each of these skits, what image or quality was the show glorifying?** For example, strong and muscular men, women with exaggerated curves and flawless skin, perfect homemakers with beautifully decorated houses, drivers of flashy cars, fashionable people, thin people, and the like.

- **What other "images" does our society glorify for people of your age?** For example, prom king/queen, jock/macho man, straight "A" student, beauty queen, cheerleader.

- **Ask yourself, without answering out loud: What is the "image" I strive to project to others? What image do I most want to exhibit or emulate?**

Alternate Warm-up: Celebrities and Heroes

Form two teams and provide each with a pencil and a sheet of paper. Give each team its assignment secretly so that the teams don't know each other's assignments.

- Team 1: make a list of the top ten most well-known or popular living people in contemporary society.

- Team 2: make a list of the top ten living people most worthy of admiration or respect, whether those people are well-known or not.

When the lists are complete, compare the lists. Ask:

- **How much overlap is there between these two lists?**

- **What is each of the ten most well-known people known for?**

- **Does their "glory" fit their "goods"? (Do they deserve national recognition and approval for what they have?)**

- **How would you rank the ten people most worthy of admiration in terms of their image and appeal?**

- **How would you rank them in terms of the worth or importance of what they're admired for?**

- **What sorts of qualities that are worth having don't "show"?**

- **How do your answers here differ from your answers for the most well-known people?**

Step 2. Defining Vainglory

Materials: *Handout 24: "Vainglory: Image Is Everything"; pencils or pens*

Distribute pens or pencils and handout 24: "Vainglory: Image Is Everything."

Have volunteers read aloud the handout, including the "faces" of vainglory in the chart. Then choose examples from the lists below and ask students to identify the categories to which the examples belong. (Obviously, you'll jump from one list to another as you give the examples.)

Faked Goods

- Embellishing stories about yourself to get attention, laughs, or approval at a party.

- Locker room talk about what you did last weekend with a girl (guy) in order to enhance your reputation.

- Paying too much attention to your appearance—complete with fake hair color, fake nails, fake eyelashes, and fake tattoo.

A *20/20* series on the seven deadly sins did a show on high school girls getting breast implants as their graduation gift. They explained that they couldn't feel good about themselves without a certain "look."

> **Tip**
>
> If you have students who are visual learners, you may want to use a large wall chart in addition to the handouts. Bring pictures of some items that fit each category and invite your group members to decide where each belongs (eg., for faked goods bring an ad for fake eyelashes).

Worthless Goods

- Thinking better of yourself because you have [insert name brand] clothing, while others shop at [name of the local thrift store]. Mocking others in the hallways with your friends or secretly looking down on them, while feeling great about yourself.

- Getting attention and friends by owning the latest or best video game system or electronic equipment.

- Adults competing with the neighbors for the lushest, greenest lawn or the best decorated house.

Stolen Goods

- Copying a paper for school off the Internet instead of writing it yourself.

- Gaining acceptance with friends (or gangs) by injuring others, stealing, vandalizing others' property, getting drunk or high.

- Lying about your high grades to your friends so that they don't alienate you for being so smart, or lying about your low grades to your parents so they think you are working harder at school than you are.

- Falsifying information on job resumes or college applications to make yourself look better than you are.

Borrowed Goods

- Receiving an award or public attention for an achievement and thinking about how great you are without ever acknowledging God as the source of your talents.

- Bragging about how many college scholarships you got, how many races/games you won or records you broke, or how much musical acclaim you received after your performance, as if it were all due to your own effort.

- Always wanting the limelight after a service project, so that everyone knows what a great Christian you are.

Invite students to suggest examples that they encounter in their own lives for each of the categories.

Step 3. What Vainglory Looks Like

Materials: *DVD of Walt Disney's* Beauty and the Beast; *DVD player and monitor; handout 25: "Christians in the Limelight"; handout 26: "Vainglory Self-Survey"; CD with song "Legacy" by Nichole Nordeman and CD player, optional*

A Study in Opposites: Gaston and Mother Teresa

Show "Gaston's Song" (DVD chapter 8) from Walt Disney's *Beauty and the Beast*. For contrast, turn immediately to handout 25: "Christians in the Limelight" and have two volunteers read aloud the parts of the interviewer and Mother Teresa.

Ask:

- **What contrasts do you see between Gaston and Mother Teresa?** Examples might include contrasts in appearance, in values, in behavior, in depth of character.

- **Whom does Gaston want to glorify? How can you tell?** Point out that vainglory seeks to glorify the self.

- **Whom does Mother Teresa want to glorify? How can you tell?**

- **Which person, Mother Teresa or Gaston, would you consider truly beautiful (worthy of attention and/or approval)? Why?** Mother Teresa's words reflect her own deep love for Christ, and also serve as a reminder to us of the beauty of a life not enslaved to the selfish attention-getting and insecure image-guarding that the vice of vainglory requires.

- **How would your life be different if you sought God's approval and praise first and foremost?**

Vainglory Self-Survey

Distribute handout 26: "Vainglory Self-Survey," and give students a few minutes to complete the survey on their own.

When students have completed the survey, follow up with questions and comments like these:

- **We have seen that vainglory is inappropriately seeking glory in some way or another.**

- **Does this mean we cannot rejoice in the good qualities and things we have been given? Not at all! We should be grateful to God for blessing us with talents and good things. The Bible teaches us that all good things are gifts from God's hand (James 1:17), and that God created us and all things good (Gen. 1). But we must remember that we are dependent upon God, the source of all our blessings, for all good things. Our lives should therefore be marked by thanksgiving, not self-congratulation, and we should never take ultimate glory in anything, but recognize it as a good gift from God.**

> **Tip**
> Play the song "Legacy" by Nichole Nordeman while students complete the survey. You can point them to the lyrics on the bottom half of handout 25: "Christians in the Limelight"

- **What's behind our addiction to this vice?** What most of us really desire is to be fully known and fully loved just as we are. Only God can perfectly fulfill this desire. Ironically, most of us spend our lives covering up who we really are and putting on a false front to impress the "right people." The pursuit of approval through vainglory leaves us insecure, unloved, and empty.

Step 4. Life Challenge: Overcoming Vainglory

Materials: *Bibles; handout 27: "Good Glory!"; handout 28: "Vanquishing Vainglory: Simple Steps and Going Further"; copies of* Celebration of Discipline *by Richard Foster, optional*

Scripture Study

Have students turn to handout 27: "Good Glory!" Work through the Scripture study there as a group, inviting volunteers to read aloud the passages listed.

Encourage students to come up with specific examples, and welcome many responses to the open-ended questions.

> **Tip**
> You can facilitate students "going further" by providing copies of Richard Foster's book *Celebration of Discipline* for your students to borrow or buy.

Daily Practice

Distribute handout 28: "Vanquishing Vainglory: Simple Steps and Going Further" and have volunteers read aloud the suggestions there. Urge students to partner with each other or agree to find others to try one of the suggestions below in the week ahead.

Close with a prayer offering all glory to God.

7

Anger: Holy Emotion or Hellish Passion?

Though we are all familiar with its sinful form, anger can also be an emotion vital to living a virtuous and holy life. As Christians we *should* be angered by some things, as the prophets were angered by the oppression of the poor and the Israelites' stubborn idolatry, for example. This "righteous indignation" or holy wrath is something God himself expresses in the Bible.

Examples of sinful anger are all around us. It is important to distinguish situations that call for holy anger from situations that tempt us to destructive wrath, and to appreciate fully the intense dangers of misguided anger.

Session Focus
Knowing how and when to get angry—righteous anger versus the sin of anger.

Session Overview

Step 1	Warm-up: Keep Your Cool or *The Mission*	Students encounter anger through an unfair game or in movie clips from *The Mission*.	Materials needed: For choice 1: 75- or 100-piece jigsaw puzzle; drinking straws; noisemakers; balloons; feathers something smelly (such as canned cat food); choice 2: DVD *The Mission*, DVD player and monitor
Step 2	Defining Anger	Students articulate definitions of anger.	Handout 29: "Holy or Hellish?"; pencils or pens
Step 3	What Anger Looks Like	Students distinguish between righteous anger and sinful anger and examine their own lives for sins of sinful anger.	Handout 30: "It's a Mad, Mad, Mad, Mad World"; handout 31: "Anger Self-Survey"
Step 4	Life Challenge: Overcoming Anger	Through studying Scripture passages and encountering specific spiritual practices, students identify ways to overcome the sin of anger in their lives.	Bibles; handout 32: "A Scripture Study in Righteous Anger"; handout 33: "Daily Practice"

Step 1. Warm-up: Keep Your Cool

In addition to the optional weekly check-in, you have two choices for a warm-up activity for this session. The first is more active and experiential, but it does require gathering a fair number of supplies. The second is also a good choice, especially if you don't have time to gather materials.

Optional: Weekly Check-in

If you wish, have students tell about their successes and challenges in doing the daily practices they committed to last week. Be sure to share your own experiences as well. If you prefer, you can do this "weekly check-in" at the end of the session.

Choice 1: "Keep Your Cool" Game

Materials: *75- or 100-piece jigsaw puzzle; drinking straws; noisemakers; balloons; feathers; something smelly (such as canned cat food)*

Recruit two contestants. Give contestant 1 the jigsaw puzzle and say, **If you complete the puzzle in the allotted time—two minutes—you will win $25.**

Then instruct the rest of the group as follows: **Your job is to distract the puzzle-makers, each in their turn, by making noises, blowing on them, tickling them lightly with feathers, rubbing or popping balloons, shooting spit-wads at them, and putting foul-smelling things in front of their noses. No touching is allowed except with feathers. Other than that, any amount of distraction is fair game.**

> **Tip**
>
> Be sure to time yourself as you assemble the puzzle yourself before this session— you want to be certain that it cannot be completed in two minutes! If the puzzle takes less than two minutes, adjust the time you allow the contestants accordingly.

Give the first contestant two minutes to attempt completion of the puzzles while the distracters do their worst. When contestant 1 fails, offer your condolences at having missed out on the prize.

Ask the group to take the puzzle apart for the next contestant. **Important!** During the commotion of taking apart the puzzle, discretely pocket one of the puzzle pieces.

Announce: **The second contestant will get double the allotted time: four minutes.**

Allow the second person to attempt the puzzle, this time for four minutes, also with distracters. If the person completes all but the last piece of the puzzle, say, ***All* pieces must be included for the contestant to win the prize money.**

During the second volunteer's attempt, be attentive to the possible complaints and anger of the first volunteer.

After the time has expired, laugh and tell them: **I had the missing piece! Did you really think I was going to give you $25?** Note the actions of the contestants and the audience carefully when they learn that the game was rigged. Listen for phrases like, "That's not fair!"

Address the following questions to the competitors, allowing time for discussion and different opinions:

- How did you feel while you were competing for the prize money?

- Did the distractions anger you as you were working on the puzzle-making task? How did you express your frustration?

- First contestant, how did you feel when I arbitrarily gave the second contestant *double* the time I gave you? How did you handle those feelings?

- Second contestant, how did you feel when I stole the last piece and cheated you out of your hard-earned prize money? How did you handle those feelings? How did you want to respond? Why did those things frustrate you the way they did?

Point out that often our anger arises from our desire for justice or fairness.

Choice 2: Movie Clips from The Mission
Materials: DVD *The Mission*, DVD player and monitor

Show DVD chapter 8, "A Brother's Death." In this scene, Rodrigo (Robert DeNiro), still in his slave-trading days, kills his brother in a jealous fight over a woman he loves and considers his own (although she is not his wife). Rodrigo is angry at his brother out of selfish motives and a desire for his own individual good, and his anger takes a destructive form, hurting two people he loves the most.

Show DVD chapter 22, "Sword in Hand." After undergoing penance for his brother's murder and becoming a priest, Rodrigo follows Father Gabriel (Jeremy Irons) to the native village above the falls. When he comes into to renounce his vows in order to take up the sword again in defense of the villagers, Father Gabriel is angry with him. His anger is in defense of God's honor. It expresses a desire to live according to love, not violence, as the example of Christ requires him to as a priest. (Catholic priests are forbidden to take up arms and shed blood, because they represent Christ.) His expression of anger is not destructive, but loving and instructive—a way of showing Christ's love to Rodrigo, the villagers, and even his enemies.

After viewing the clips, ask questions like these:
- **Why is Rodrigo angry in the first clip?**

- **What does he desire? Why?**

- **Whose good is he most concerned with?**

- **What is the effect of his anger on the others around him?**

- **Does his anger express love?**

- **Why is Father Gabriel angry in the second clip?**

- **What does he desire? Why?**

- **Whose good is he most concerned with?**

- **What is the effect of his anger on the others around him?**

- **Does his anger express love?**

Step 2. Defining Anger

Materials: *Handout 29: "Anger: Holy or Hellish?"; pencils or pens*

Distribute pens or pencils and handout 29: "Anger: Holy or Hellish?" Invite volunteers to read aloud the quotes and statements on the handout. Then challenge each person to write his or her own definition of anger as a sin in the space provided under "Definitions."

Have students share their responses.

Step 3. What Anger Looks Like

Materials: *Handout 30: "It's a Mad, Mad, Mad, Mad World"; handout 31: "Anger Self-Survey"*

Holy or Hellish?

Direct students to handout 30: "It's a Mad, Mad, Mad, Mad World."

Form pairs or trios and designate half of the pairs as *"What Assessors"* and the other half, *"How Assessors."* Give these instructions:

- *What* **Assessors: Working with your partner or trio, circle each of the scenarios below in which the person gets the "what" of anger wrong. If you're not certain, look at the chart at the top of the sheet and at the two questions on handout 29.**

- *How* **Assessors: Working with your partner or trio, circle each of the scenarios below in which the person gets the "how" of anger wrong. If you're not certain, look at the chart at the top of the sheet and at the two questions on handout 29.**

When most pairs have finished their assessments, bring them back together to explain their answers to the other groups.

Debrief with some of the following questions as appropriate, depending on which scenarios you examined:

- **In which of the scenarios you looked at is anger self-seeking (it's all about what I want) instead of serving justice?**

- **In which scenarios is anger a tool for getting our own way instead of making things right and resisting wrong?**

- **Do any examples show how love can motivate anger?**

- **Do any examples show how hatred and pride can motivate anger?**

- **How could an example of seeking revenge (from one of the scenarios) be changed to serve justice, or vice versa?**

> ## Tip
>
> If you have only 45 minutes for your session, you won't be able to do all the activities given in this session. To save time in step 3, use one of these options:
>
> - Assign and discuss only a few of the scenarios.
> - If you have enough pairs, assign different scenarios to different pairs. For example, one pair of "**What** Assessors" could examine all the odd-numbered scenarios and another pair of "**What** Assessors" could examine all the even-numbered scenarios. Remember that you need at least one "What" and one "How" pair for each scenario you wish to assess.

- In which of the scenarios could the people be described as having "short fuses and hot heads"—anger too intense or vehement (disproportionate to the offense), or too quickly aroused?

- In which of the scenarios are the people nursing a grudge, staying angry at the person even after the score is settled?

- What examples do you see of taking things too personally—wanting revenge, rather than simply righting a wrong?

Sum up the activity by saying, **Anger can be an appropriate and righteous emotion when it is**
- **motivated by love and**

- **serves justice.**

Anger Self-Survey

Distribute handout 31: "Anger Self-Survey" and give students a few minutes to complete the survey on their own.

When students have completed the survey, have volunteers read aloud the quotes at the bottom of the page. Ask, **Do you think these quotes apply only to vicious anger (hellish wrath) or also to virtuous anger (holy emotion)? Why?**

Tip

If your students are open to it, use examples from their own experiences instead of the scenarios on the student handout. Solicit examples from students' own experience by asking questions like these:
- When were you last angry?
- When were you most angry?

As volunteers are willing, have them assess the "what" and the "how" to determine whether the anger was righteous anger or not.

Step 4. Life Challenge: Overcoming Anger

Materials: *Bibles; handout 32: "A Scripture Study in Righteous Anger; handout 33: "Daily Practice"*

Scripture Study: Getting Angry as God Does

Have students look at handout 32: "A Scripture Study in Righteous Anger."

Form pairs or trios and divide up the passages among them. Allow a few minutes for each pair to read their passages and summarize them in writing on their handouts. Then bring everyone together to report.

- **What does God get angry about?** Sin. Examples from the passages include idolatry, arrogance, pride, disobedience, oppressing the poor, injustice, blasphemy.

- **Advice on How (NOT) to Get Angry: O.T.** Fear God; don't be hot-headed; give a gentle answer; speak with restraint; choose friends who can control their anger; control yourself; don't stir up arguments.

- **Advice on How (NOT) to Get Angry: N.T.** Don't call people names; love; don't let the sun go down on your anger; be quick to listen and slow to speak.

- **Patterning Our Anger After God's.** The LORD is "slow to anger and abounding in steadfast love."

- **What does Jesus get angry about?** Although we know that Jesus was angry about sin many times, the only time the word anger is applied to him is when the Pharisees try to use the Sabbath law to prevent Jesus from healing someone.

After all the pairs have reported, ask:

- **What does the biblical pattern of God's anger teach us about God?**

- **What does Christ's example teach us about the WHAT and HOW of righteous anger?**

- **How should Christians express their anger?**

- **Should Christians be known as angry people?**

- **How can we respond adequately to injustice and sin without falling into the habit of vicious anger?** As Christians we must be careful not to let even our justified anger lead to unjust violence, nor should we let anger consume us. Even while we do all that we can now to seek justice and bring shalom to a fallen world, we also need to rest in the firm confidence that God is in control and will bring final justice in the last day. In other words, even in our righteous anger, we should not presume to play God. On the other hand, those suffering injustice in the world should arouse our passion and keep us from resignation or apathy. Keeping LOVE at the root of our anger is the key.

Daily Practice

Distribute handout 33: "Daily Practice in Confronting and Controlling Anger" and have volunteers read aloud the suggestions there. Urge students to partner with each other or agree to find others to try one of the suggestions below in the week ahead.

Close with prayer.

8

Lust:
The All-Consuming Fire

Many Christians simply equate vice with lust. Sexual sins have special weight in the church because of the deep personal and social consequences that accompany immoral sexual activity and because of the promiscuity of the media and the culture. As a result, young people may find it especially difficult to balance warnings about sexual immorality with an affirming view of sexual desire and activity as a gift created beautiful by God.

In this session we will examine sexuality as a God-given gift and look at the sinful distortions of sexual desire and pleasure that count as lust.

Session Focus
Embracing the proper expression of sexual desire rather than falling prey to the empty promises of lustful pleasures.

Session Overview

Step 1	Warm-up: The Big Flame	Students encounter either a biblical perspective of healthy love and sexuality or its opposite in various media.	Materials needed: For choice 1: NOOMA DVD: "Flame," DVD player and monitor; choice 2: magazines and/or current CDs and CD player; handout 34: "She No Longer Brought Him Pleasure"
Step 2	Defining Lust	Students articulate definitions of lust.	Handout 35: "A Four-Letter Word"; pencils or pens
Step 3	What Lust Looks Like	Through Bible study, discussion, and object lesson, students reflect on the harm that lust causes.	Board or newsprint; chalk or marker; Bibles; duct tape; scissors; handout 36: "Just a Rental?"; handout 37: "Confessions of a Porn Addict"
Step 4	Life Challenge: Overcoming Lust	Students identify specific ways to overcome the sin of lust in their lives.	Bible; CD with song "Your Body Is a Wonderland" by John Mayer; CD player; handout 38: "Your Body Is a Wonderland"; handout 39: "Daily Practice: Controlling the Fire"

Step 1. Warm-up: The Big Flame

In additional to the optional weekly check-in, you have two choices for a warm-up activity for this session. The first uses a NOOMA film; the second incorporates a variety magazines and/or music CDs.

Optional: Weekly Check-in

If you wish, have students tell about their successes and challenges in doing the daily practices they committed to last week. Be sure to share your own experiences as well. If you prefer, you can do this "weekly check-in" at the end of the session.

Choice 1: "Flame"
Materials: *NOOMA DVD "Flame"; DVD player and monitor*

Introduce the DVD by saying something like this: **Sexual desire is like fire. It is a great and powerful thing—beautiful and useful when its power is honored, dangerous and destructive when we misuse it or are careless about it. We are going to get a picture of the power and beauty of sexual desire through the help of a short film entitled "Flame."**

Play the DVD. (It will take 11 minutes.)

Choice 2: Media Is the Message
Materials: *Magazines and/or current CDs and CD player; handout 34: "She No Longer Brought Him Pleasure"*

If you prefer, use this warm-up activity instead of the DVD option.

Provide a variety of magazines and ask students to look through them, focusing on advertisements and other images. Or listen to songs that talk about sex, relationships, or sexual themes.

Ask:

- **What is the message** [in an individual example] **of the way women ought to be? The way men ought to be?**

- **What role does sexuality play in this example?**

- **What is the image of the relationships between men and women? What does this tell us we can expect from our romantic and sexual relationships?**

- **What do these examples teach us about how to be accepted by the opposite sex, or how to be desirable to the opposite sex?**

- **What impact, if any, do you think these media messages might have on people?**

- **How can we "see through" those messages instead of allowing ourselves to be "shaped by" them? Can you give some examples of media messages you can "see through"?**

> **Tip**
> "Flame" is part of a series of short films in DVD format called NOOMA. They are published by Zondervan and are readily available online (www.nooma.com) and in your local Christian bookstore.

> **Tip**
> Use caution in choosing magazines. The content of magazines like **Cosmopolitan**, **Marie Claire**, **Maxim**, and **GQ** effectively illustrates the lies the media tells about sex and lust, but may be inappropriate for your group. Other magazines such as **People**, **Sports Illustrated**, and **Glamour** can be just as effective, but not so offensive.

> **Tip**
> If you think your students will be unduly embarrassed by the frank language in the poem, have them read it silently rather than aloud, or skip the poem altogether.

Distribute handout 34: "She No Longer Brought Him Pleasure" and have a male and female volunteer read the stanzas as an illustration of the expectations the media can raise.

Step 2. Defining Lust

Materials: *Handout 35: "A Four-Letter Word"; pencils or pens*

Hand out pencils or pens and direct students' attention to handout 35: "A Four-Letter Word."

Have volunteers read aloud the quotes on the handout. Then ask, **How would you give a contemporary paraphrase of these definitions? Take a minute to write out your own definition in the space provided.**

When most people have written something, ask students to share their definitions.

Step 3. What Lust Looks Like

Step 3 offers more activities than you will have time for in a single session. Choose those that best meet the needs of your group.

Smoke Damage

Materials: *Board or newsprint; chalk or marker*

Introduce the next portion of the session with comments like these:
- **Lust may be one of the seven deadly sins that people think feels good. Nobody wants to feel envious or angry, but lust can seem kind of fun. And a lot of people would argue that it doesn't hurt anybody.**

- **But let's compare sexual desire to a fire again. When a fire gets out of control, it can create a lot of smoke damage, even in things and people who stay out of the flame itself.**

- **Sexual desire that gets out of hand doesn't just damage those who have it, but also those who are close to that person and the whole community.**

Ask students if they can think of examples of ways that lust hurts others. Write them on your board or newsprint. Emphasize examples that affect not just the persons directly involved, but the whole community. Supplement student responses with the following examples if you choose:
- No one wants a paroled sex offender living in the neighborhood—that person's previous sexual sin feels like a threat to the community.

- Pornographic media fills our minds with sexual violence and fantasy and hurts our ability to respect all members of the opposite sex.

- Sexual harassment can create environments where many others feel threatened just because they are of a certain sex.

- Premarital sex hurts our future marriage partner and creates peer pressure for others who are trying to stay chaste.

- Billboards and magazines expose children to sexual content.

- Extramarital affairs and sexual abuse can rip whole families and churches apart.

Scripture Study: How Lust Damages Others
Materials: *Bibles*

Read or briefly summarize the story of David and Bathsheba (2 Samuel 11), or have a student do so. Discuss it with the following comments and questions:

- **The fires of lust consumed more than just the lustful person in the story of King David. This is a story about the "collateral damage" to a wide range of human relationships caused by the lust of a single person.**

- **Who was affected by David's desires when they burned out of control? Possible answers include the following:**

  - Uriah, a loyal soldier of the king's, was murdered and his loyalty to his wife, his king, and comrades was betrayed.

  - Bathsheba was widowed.

  - The child born to Bathsheba and David died, leaving both of them in grief.

  - The generals of the army and the messengers were lied to, damaging trust between them and their leader.

  - The whole community saw its trusted leader immersed in shame and disgrace (via the prophet Nathan's expose).

  - David's relationship with God was marred by the brokenness of sin (see Ps. 51).

In the course of the discussion, make sure the following points come out:
- **Sexual desire is designed by God to accompany and strengthen the bond of love in marriage. Sexual union and its natural pleasure help this relationship of love to flourish.**

- **Lust, on the other hand, breaks human relationships. It creates a life dedicated to immediate, selfish gratification, rather than self-giving love. Through David's lust, many relationships of love and trust were damaged and even destroyed.**

Have a volunteer read aloud 1 Thessalonians 4:1-7. Ask:
- **What kinds of things does this passage say should be off-limits for Christians?** This passage doesn't prohibit only sexual intercourse itself. It prohibits *all* forms of sexual immorality and impurity—any lustful desires or actions that exploit our brothers and sisters—so that we do not wrong others or take advantage of them in any way.

- **Why do you think that's important?** Lust can even destroy the relationship in which it begins. Rather than bringing people together, as sexual desire was designed to do, lust's desire for self-gratification works its way out of your imagination and private thoughts to destroy your ability to love others. These limits protect and respect something good—your good and the good of others.

Don't Get Burned: How Lust Hurts You
Materials: *Duct tape; scissors*

Say: **Often people believe the myth that their secret porn habit or their private sex with a willing partner is perfectly justifiable and not harmful to anyone. Duct tape is a good visual aid to help us show this idea to be false.**

Give everyone about a foot-long (about .3 m) strip of duct tape. Set aside a similar strip for use later. Then give these instructions:
- **Stick your piece of duct tape to another person's duct tape and then peel the pieces back apart.**

- **Now do the same thing with at least three other pieces, or to other objects like the carpet or clothing.**

When all the duct tape has been stuck and unstuck several times, ask:
- **How did your duct tape look before this exercise?**

- **How does your duct tape look after this exercise? Has it lost its stickiness? Are there piece missing or crumpled? Is it worn out? Is there any way to make it sticky again?**

- **In what way could this activity be like hooking up with one sexual partner after another?** This piece of duct tape represents our ability to bond sexually with another person. We have been made by God with the desire and ability to "stick" together with someone else. We will retain the strongest bonding power if we (and our spouses) have never stuck to anyone else before. This exercise illustrates the internal damage lust does to us. Most people think they can walk away intact, but in reality they carry the damage done around with him or her the rest of their lives.

Now draw attention to the piece of duct tape you set aside and didn't stick to anything. Say: **Imagine that this represents your spouse, who kept him- or herself pure. How does your premarital duct-tape sticking affect him or her? Rather than keeping your full ability to bond to this special person, your lustful desire and activity has damaged your ability to bond and unite with this person too. If you care about this person, the hurt you cause him or her will hurt you too.**

Thought Starters
Materials: *Handout 36: "Just a Rental?"; handout 37: "Confessions of a Porn Addict")*

If you have students who respond well to reading and discussing an article, you may wish to simply read and talk about the material on handout 36 "Just a Rental?" and/or handout 37: "Confessions of a Porn Addict" instead of the other activities in this step.

If you don't use these handouts during the session, send them home with students to read on their own if they wish.

Step 4. Life Challenge: Overcoming Lust

Materials: *Bible; CD with song "Your Body Is a Wonderland" by John Mayer; CD player; handout 38: "Your Body Is a Wonderland"; handout 39: "Daily Practice: Controlling the Fire"*

Amusement Park or Holy Temple?

Distribute handout 38: "Your Body Is a Wonderland" and play the chorus of the song while students follow the lyrics on the handout.

Ask:

- **Why do you go to an amusement park?** Expect responses such as "cheap thrills," "fun," and "entertainment."

- **How long do you stay at an amusement park?** Guide students to recognize that you can leave whenever you've had enough or you're sick of it.

- **Do you care about keeping it clean and well-maintained?**

- **How does this picture—of bodies as sexual wonderlands or "amusement parks" for others—encourage us to think about others?**

> **Tip**
>
> Instead of listening to the song on CD, you could show the clip from the episode "A Benihana Christmas" from season 3 (2006) of **The Office**, where Michael and Andy sing "Your Body Is a Wonderland" to the waitresses they picked up at Benihana. If you don't have the CD or **The Office** DVD, you can simply read the lyrics aloud.

Have a volunteer read 1 Corinthians 6:18-20, which calls our bodies temples of the Holy Spirit. Ask:

- **What's the difference between thinking of your body—or someone else's—as an amusement park (a "wonderland") and thinking of your body as God's holy temple (a sacred place)?**

- **How does knowing God sees your body as sacred space make you feel?**

Remind students that God designed our bodies to give and receive sexual pleasure to accompany and strengthen the bond of love in marriage. Sexual union and its natural pleasure help this relationship of love to flourish.

Point students to the "Love Versus Lust Litany" at the bottom of the handout. Have one half of the group (or one student) read the "love" lines, and the second half (or a second student) read the "lust" lines.

Daily Practice

Direct students to handout 39: "Daily Practice: Controlling the Fire," and have volunteers read aloud the suggestions there. Urge students to partner with each other or agree to find others to try one of the suggestions below in the week ahead.

Close with prayer.

9

Gluttony:
Feeding Your Face and
Starving Your Heart

Many people commonly misunderstood gluttony as merely overeating and becoming overweight. The vice of gluttony, however, appears in many forms and may not have anything to do with one's weight. Gluttony, like the other vices, involves spiritual harm that often greatly outweighs any unhealthy physical behaviors.

The desire to eat is a normal, healthy, God-given part of being human. Gluttony distorts this natural appetite into an excessive desire for pleasure and self-gratification.

Session Focus
Moving from gluttony's self-gratification to genuine gratitude in our eating habits.

Session Overview

Step 1	Warm-up: Eating Habits	Students encounter various forms of gluttony through skits.	Materials needed: Copy of "Eating Habits Skit Instructions" (p. 71) cut apart; popcorn or other food; plates
Step 2	Defining Gluttony	Students articulate definitions of gluttony.	Handout 40: "Gluttony: Feeding Your Face and Starving Your Heart"; pencils or pens
Step 3	What Gluttony Looks Like	Students identify examples of gluttony in case studies and in their own lives.	Handout 41: "Gluttony Self-Survey"
Step 4	Life Challenge: Overcoming Gluttony	Through studying Scripture passages and encountering specific spiritual practices, students identify ways to overcome the sin of gluttony in their lives.	Handout 42: "A Biblical Perspective on Gluttony"; handout 43: "The Spiritual Discipline of Fasting"; military "Meal Ready to Eat" and scissors to open the meal, optional

Step 1. Warm-up: Skits

Materials: *Copy of "Eating Habits Skit Instructions" (p. 71) cut apart; popcorn or other food; plates*

Optional: Weekly Check-in

If you wish, have students tell about their successes and challenges in doing the daily practices they committed to last week. Be sure to share your own experiences as well. If you prefer, you can do this "weekly check-in" at the end of the session.

Eating Habits Skits

Recruit five volunteers to act out short scenes. Give each volunteer one of the sections from the cut-apart copy of "Eating Habits Skit Instructions" and ask them to review their instructions carefully.

Explain to the rest of the group, **Each volunteer will act out a type of gluttonous eating. Watch and decide why their eating could be called a form of gluttony.**

Set out plates and food as follows:

- Set a plate with a moderate amount of food in front of volunteer 1, who will eat *too fussily.*

- Set out three plates each with food (labeled with the three different brands) in front of volunteer 2, who will eat *too richly.*

- Set down lots of food in front of volunteer 3, who will eat *too much.*

- Set a moderate amount of food in front of volunteer 4, who will eat *too soon and too hastily.*

- Set a lot of food in front of volunteer 5. Have extra food somewhere else in the room. This volunteer will eat *too greedily.*

> **Tip**
>
> The food you provide for this skit can be as simple as popcorn or as elaborate as a different kind of food for each skit. For example, you might use Oreos for eating too fussily, Jif peanut butter for eating too richly, marshmallows for eating too much, popcorn for eating too hastily, pudding or something else that can be messy for eating too greedily.

Allow the volunteers to act out their form of gluttony, one at a time.

When all of the volunteers have demonstrated their manner of eating, debrief the exercise with the following comments and questions:

- **We often associate gluttony with just overeating. But as our skits have showed us, gluttony has many different forms.**

- **How would you describe the gluttony we saw in the first skit?** Student may describe the gluttony in a variety of ways, but draw out the notion of eating *too fussily.*

- **How would you describe the gluttony we saw in the second skit?** Eating *too richly.*

- **The third?** Eating *too much.*

- **The fourth?** Eating *too soon and too hastily.*

- **And the fifth?** Eating *too greedily.*

Explain that you'll explore how each of those ways of eating can be a form of gluttony.

Step 2. Defining Gluttony

Materials: *Handout 40: "Gluttony: Feeding Your Face and Starving Your Heart"; pencils and pens*

Distribute pencils or pens and handout 40: "Gluttony: Feeding Your Face and Starving Your Heart."

Invite volunteers to read aloud the various quotes on the handout. After a volunteer has read the section headed, "Five Forms of Gluttony," ask:

- **How does each of these forms of gluttony express an excessive desire for the pleasure of eating?**

- **Do any of these forms of gluttony look familiar to you from your own life?**

When you have read all the quotes on the handout, give students a few minutes to work independently and write their own definitions in the space with the sentence-starter, "Gluttony is . . ."

When most people are done, have students share their definitions. Reinforce the following points:

- **Philippians 3:17-21 teaches that when we make gluttony a habit, our stomachs become our gods (idols). We let eating— its comfort, pleasure, and fullness—rule our lives and take the place of seeking and finding our fulfillment in God.**

- **In 1 Corinthians 6:12, Paul describes vices like gluttony and lust in terms of being "mastered by pleasure," so that getting *my* desires satisfied becomes my number-one priority.**

Tip
The question of eating disorders such as anorexia or bulimia may come up in connection with your session on gluttony. If so, you'll want to explain that eating disorders are indeed the result of sin and are related to inner needs. True healing must involve finding the fulfillment of those needs in God. But be sure students understand that we can't blame the person with anorexia for her problem, not can we "cure" her by urging her to repent.

Step 3. What Gluttony Looks Like

Materials: *Handout 41: "Gluttony Self-Survey"*

Gluttony or Not?

Read aloud the following cases, asking students to determine whether each example does or does not illustrate gluttony. If you wish, make it a game by having two teams compete for the highest number of right answers. Keep a running tally of points on the board for all to see.

You may also have groups identify which of the five forms of gluttony are at issue in each case, in addition to determining whether or not it is case of gluttony.

Case 1: Here comes Mrs. Davis. She's thirty years old and eats five large meals a day. In addition, she has a snack every two hours between meals. Gluttony or not?

Tip
If time does not permit discussing them all, select a sample of the stories below. Choose examples that are most appropriate or challenging for your students. Feel free to invent and discuss your own (or the students' own) examples if you wish. (For instance: "I only drink Diet"; complaining about cafeteria food or your mom's cooking; grabbing a second helping on the first time through the buffet line to make sure you don't miss out on the good stuff.)

Field answers—if you like, take an initial vote (or team vote)—and then ask for reasons why one would or would not call her actions gluttonous. Repeat this process for each case study you use.

After some discussion time, tell the real story of Mrs. Davis:
Mrs. Davis is pregnant with twins. Her doctor recommended that she increase her eating habits for the purpose of having healthy babies, so her behavior is motivated by a concern for her own health and the health of others, not an excessive desire for the pleasure of eating.

Answer: Not gluttony.

Case 2: Here comes Mike. He is forty-eight years old and he eats three meals a day. Each meal he eats consists of an astounding number of calories and is usually enough to feed two people. Gluttony or not?

Field answers, take votes, then ask for reasons why. Then tell the real story:
Mike is a professional landscaper. He spends all day lifting and moving rock, brick, dirt, and plants. He works hard and needs all the calories he can get. He is 6'3" and is not at all overweight for his height. Again, health, not pleasure, drives his eating habits.

Answer: Not gluttony.

Case 3: Here comes nine-year-old Jonathan. He is very fit and strong, and he usually eats very healthfully for a kid his age. When he eats a sandwich for lunch, Jonathan insists on having Jif peanut butter on it. (His mom is a choosy mom.) He refuses peanut butter-and-jelly sandwiches at his cousins' house because they use the generic store brand. Gluttony or not?

Field answers, take votes, then ask for reasons why.
Jonathan is too picky! He has no real reason to be picky, but he insists on eating only the top quality brand. Nothing else tastes good enough. Our healthy little guy is guilty of eating "too richly."

Answer: Gluttony.

Case 4: Here comes Kendra. She is sixteen years old and is the heaviest girl in the junior class at Central High. Her doctor has worked in the past with her at trying to keep her weight down at normal levels. Gluttony or not?

Field answers, take votes, then ask for reasons why. Tell the real story.
Kendra has a medical condition that affects her thyroid gland. She was diagnosed with a glandular malfunction at the age of fourteen, and it has drastically changed her metabolism in ways medication cannot control.

Answer: Not gluttony.

Case 5: Here comes Bob. A high school senior, he is very unpopular. Bob spends much of his school day alone and rarely has friends to do things with in the evenings. You can usually find him after dinner watching TV with a bag of Doritos. Both help distract him from his feelings of misery. Gluttony or not?

Field answers, take votes, then ask for reasons why.

Bob's case is an example of eating "comfort foods" in order to cover over or avoid deeper pain or difficulty. The food is desired only for the immediate pleasure and the way it drowns out other things one doesn't want to face. We might be sympathetic toward Bob and his problems, but distracting himself with food is no solution at all.

Answer: Gluttony

Case 6: **Here comes Joe, a very popular high school senior. He is busy all the time: hanging out with friends, working as a lifeguard, and being captain of the soccer team. When he's home for dinner, he sits hunched over his plate, eating steadily without really engaging in conversation. He's the one at McDonald's who always interrupts to ask, "Are you going to finish that?" And frankly, he gets pretty impatient when the social life at youth group is better than the food served. Gluttony or not?**

Field answers, take votes, then ask for reasons why.

While Joe seems to have a lot going for him in general, he consistently seems more concerned about what there is for him to eat rather than about the people he is with. It seems backwards to value the pleasure of eating more than enjoying time spent with other people. Joe puts his own pleasure above concern for others, even when his health is not threatened.

Answer: Gluttony.

Case 7: **Here comes Karen. She is preparing an elaborate meal for her family and friends, consisting of filet mignon, several of the choicest wines, caviar, various imported cheeses, four different kinds of desserts including a $500 cake, and so on. She spends over a month planning and preparing the meal, and she exceeds her monthly food budget by over $5,000. Gluttony or not?**

Field answers, take votes, then ask for reasons why. Tell the real story.

Karen's only son just returned with minor wounds from a year of dangerous military service and is getting married this weekend. She is preparing a feast to celebrate his safe return and the wedding. While the food, and her concern with it, might be excessive under ordinary circumstances, the feasting seems appropriate considering the extraordinariness of the day and the celebration. (Remember Jesus' first miracle!)

Answer: Not gluttony.

Case 8: **Here comes short, skinny five-year-old Beth. She is the youngest child in her family, and she thinks that means she is always getting the short end of the stick. She comes into the kitchen at 5 p.m. No one else is around. Seizing her chance, she drags a chair over to the cookie jar on the counter and helps herself to a hefty five-cookie snack, leaving nothing for the rest of the family's lunches tomorrow. Gluttony or not?**

Field answers, take votes, then ask for reasons why.

Beth goes for the triple slam—eating too soon (before the dinner hour), too much (five cookies instead of one or two), and too greedily (in a way that does not leave enough for

others). She might also be eating too fast to make sure she has those cookies gone before anyone else walks in.

Answer: Gluttony.

Case 9: Here comes Shane, a nineteen-year-old freshman in college who eats three meals a day. He occasionally snacks and enjoys ice-cream sundaes. Gluttony or not?

Field answers, take votes, then ask for reasons why.
For this last one, I am not going to tell you the real story. As you know by now, gluttony cannot always be seen from the outside. In this case, as in your own life, the challenge is to evaluate your internal desires as well as outward behavior.

Sum up the activity with the following comments:
- **The point of this activity is that our stereotypes about gluttony don't always apply. The vice of gluttony is *less* concerned with the quantity of food or how frequently we eat or the physical appearance of the eater, and *more* concerned with the way we give excessive love and attention to the pleasures of eating and drinking, especially when we seek these pleasures over other legitimate goods.**

- **As these cases illustrate, our disordered desires for the pleasure of food can show themselves in many different ways; diagnosing gluttony may be not be as simple as we think.**

Gluttony Self-Survey
Have students turn to handout 41: "Gluttony Self-Survey." Allow a few minutes for them to work independently to complete the self-survey on the handout.

Tip
After the students are done filling out their survey, ask if anyone would be willing to share some of their answers and conclusions (especially for the first two questions) with the group.

Step 4. Life Challenge: Overcoming Gluttony
Materials: *Handout 42: "A Biblical Perspective on Gluttony"; handout 43: "The Spiritual Discipline of Fasting"; military "Meal Ready to Eat" and scissors to open the meal, optional*

If you have an hour or less for your session, you'll need to pick and choose among the activities and options offered in step 4. Choose those that best meet the needs of your group.

Scripture Study: A Biblical Perspective on Gluttony
Distribute handout 42: "A Biblical Perspective on Gluttony." Form pairs of students, and have partners work together to summarize the message of each passage and write their summaries in the spaces provided.

After the pairs have had an adequate time to summarize each text, go through them one by one.
Ask: **How do these verses help us see the difference between gluttony and a rightly ordered view of the pleasure and place of food in our lives?**

Optional: Going Deeper

If time permits, you may wish to read and discuss the following additional Bible passages and ideas:

- Discuss God's provision of manna in the desert (Exodus 16) and the petition in the Lord's Prayer for daily bread (Luke 11:3).

- What do the stories in 1 Kings 17 (the widow of Zarephath) and Luke 9:10-17 (feeding of the five thousand) teach us about how much food is enough? Is our excessive desire for food linked to a lack of daily reliance on God?

- Read the story of Jesus changing water into wine at the wedding feast (John 2:1-11). What is the significance of this first miracle for the place of eating and drinking, and its enjoyment, in the kingdom of God? Why do you think the coming of God's kingdom often represented as a banquet or feast (in the Gospels and in Revelation)?

- Read about Jesus' first temptation in the desert (Matthew 4:1-13). Why was changing stones into bread one of the temptations, and why did Jesus refuse it? What is the role of fasting in the life of a disciple of Christ? See Luke 5:33-39 and Matthew 6:16-18. Does fasting undervalue the pleasure of eating and drinking the way gluttony overvalues it, or is there a difference?

- Reflect on the Last Supper (Matthew 26:17-30; Mark 14:12-26; Luke 22:7-23) and the early church's fellowship practices (Acts 2:42-47). Why do you think the main sacrament of the Christian church centers on eating and drinking? How did the early believers eat and drink "with due regard for others" (as Augustine recommends)?

Optional Object Lesson: MRE ("Meal Ready to Eat")

Show students the MRE—"Meal Ready to Eat." Cut it open. As you pass around the contents, read the following:

When a United States military unit is in combat or on a mission, they bring along "Meals Ready to Eat" or MREs. These are individual meals for soldiers. They have some unique and interesting special properties. Each meal contains approximately 1,200 calories and includes

- **an entrée or starch;**

- **crackers and a cheese, peanut butter, or jelly spread;**

- **a dessert or snack;**

- **beverage;**

- **an accessory packet;**

- **plastic silverware;**

- **and a flameless ration heater (FRH).**

> ### Tip
> "Meals Ready to Eat" are available at Army Navy surplus stores or online (Google "Meals Ready to Eat").

Research and development breakthroughs have made it possible for MREs to be lightweight, compact, and easy to open. They can withstand a parachute drop from about 1,200 feet, or from a helicopter at 100 feet with no parachute. They can also endure inclement weather and survive temperature extremes from minus 60 degrees Fahrenheit to 120 degrees Fahrenheit. They have a minimum shelf life of three years at 80 degrees Fahrenheit; some can last up to thirty years.

The MRE is a totally self-contained, flexibly-packaged meal used by U.S. Army personnel and Marines in the field. It is used to sustain individuals during operations that prevent organized food service facilities but where resupply is established or planned. These meals—while not exactly gourmet fare—are designed to supply enough energy and sustenance to complete the task at hand.

The box with the entrée often has a chart on it: FOOD → Energy → Top Performance. The clear goal of the meal is to nourish soldiers so that they can carry out their assigned operations effectively and successfully. Soldiers are always aware of the fact that their mission is more important than the pleasure of their meal. For this reason the food is cooked over a flameless heater, so as to not give away the unit's position. Moreover, soldiers are ready and able to give up their MREs altogether or eat them cold, if the mission demands it.

Make the following comments:
- Soldiers on the field of combat eat in order to carry out their mission. Their physical good and their disciplined training serve a greater purpose or goal. As it says on the package: food → energy → performance. By contrast, gluttons eat only for pleasure, without regard for their own greater good or for the good of others.

- Soldiers subordinate their own pleasure to the mission and their role in it, if necessary. By contrast, gluttons make their own pleasure and gratification the sole objective.

> ## Tip
> For maximum impact, cook and eat the MRE together.

- Just as soldiers are trained and disciplined to eat in ways that help them carry out their mission, as Christians, we too are on a mission—a spiritual mission. Food and its pleasures can detract from our task to serve God if we make them more important than the good of that mission.

- Sometimes a meal can help to reinforce our identity and mission. Even in Iraq marines get a giant cake on the birthday of the marine corp. Similarly, the Lord's Supper is an occasion of eating and drinking that confirms our identity and mission.

Ask:
- What is your spiritual mission? Becoming like Jesus Christ? Serving the world in love?

- How do your present desires for the pleasure of eating and drinking help or hinder you in that mission?

If you have time, you may wish to continue the discussion using some or all of the following questions.
- How does our preoccupation with the pleasure of eating interfere with our mission to live godly lives?

- When we've overstuffed ourselves, do we feel like going out and serving others or resting on the couch?

- When we are too eager to get the best piece of cake, what does this attitude say about our concern for putting others first or noticing their needs?

- If we typically eat foods that are really bad for us just because they taste good (sugary, sweet, fatty), what does that say about our love for ourselves and our respect for our bodies?

- If we are at someone else's house for dinner and pick through the food on our plates and leave most of it as unfit to eat, what does this say about our gratitude and courtesy toward others?

- Does our pleasure in food make us content, or does it leave us wanting more and better? How much of our lives is consumed with eating or planning or wanting to eat?

- When we are busy, do we have more or less desire to eat?

- What is the right balance of these activities in our lives?

- What do all of these eating habits say about the centrality of our spiritual mission and the place of food in it? Is our eating and drinking enhancing our mission or detracting from it?

Make sure that students grasp the point of this analogy between military and spiritual discipline: that eating delicious, nourishing food—even feasting—is not only permissible but good, if and when it doesn't distract us from our assigned "operations" as faithful disciples of Christ.

Optional: Family Practice

Share the following story:

> A Nigerian student once told a story of the eating practices in his household. The family always gave the oldest child the largest helping of food. This may sound like a great deal for the oldest child, but the largest helping came with the following responsibility: the oldest child had to eat slowly enough that he or she let the younger children finish their portions first. Then, if any of the younger children were still hungry, the oldest child had to share some of his or her larger portion.

Ask:
- How might this dinner table practice help counteract our temptation to gluttony?

- Does it differ from interactions at the dinner table in your family? How?

The Spiritual Discipline of Fasting

Direct students' attention to handout 43: "The Spiritual Discipline of Fasting," and invite volunteers to read it aloud.

Then ask:
- Under what circumstances could you abstain from food readily and uncomplainingly for the sake of the kingdom?
- On a scale of 1-5, with 1 being easy and 5 being impossible, rate how hard would it be to give up the following:
  - soda
  - sugary foods (snacks, desserts, sugar cereal, chocolate)
  - snacking for a day—or a week—or even a month

Tell students that in the Middle Ages, Christians living in monasteries often ate only one meal a day (at around 3 p.m.) as a regular part of a life dedicated to God. This level of discipline is not impossible!

- **Would it be easier to "abstain from food readily and uncomplainingly" if this were something we practiced regularly?**

Challenge students to give up soda, sugar, or snacks as a life experiment for one week. Encourage them to find partners with whom they can discuss their experiences.

Close with a prayer for grace and discipline in applying the lessons learned throughout this course.

Eating Habits Skit Instructions

1. Eating too fussily

Your job is to eat only one piece of food. You should not, however, eat it as you normally would, but you should eat it "too fussily." Approach the food very dramatically. Be very vocal in your evaluation of it. "Oh, I love this part here!" Break off any parts that don't look appealing, saying, "Eeew, I can't eat this part—it's too burnt" (or hard, or whatever applies). As you do all this, smell, feel, and touch the food. Take very small bites and savor them, closing your eyes and sighing with enjoyment.

2. Eating too richly

Your job is to eat from only one of the three plates of food. Examine the food on all three plates, saying aloud the brand names. First, evaluate what seems to be the cheapest brand. "Gross—I would never eat that brand!" Then examine the second plate, again voicing a critical attitude about it. Mock this food, saying how this brand makes inferior food.

Finally, look at the third plate. In an uppity tone, examine the food and tell everyone what good quality this brand is, how pure and exclusive the special ingredients are, and how this is the only one you with your sensitive palate will eat. Eat the food from the third plate.

3. Eating too much

It is your task to eat as much as you can. Speed is not important. Eat one piece of the food slowly and then say, "Wow! This is delicious!" Then eat a second, and say, "That was delicious too!" Keep eating, saying something after each piece that you eat. Eventually, say, "Just one more." "Wow! I'm really full—but this tastes so good!" "One more couldn't hurt." "Mmmm, delicious! Just one more."

4. Eating too soon or too hastily

Try to sneak some of your food before it's time for your part of the skit. When it's time to start, say, "Oops! I already ate some. I couldn't help myself. It's too hard to wait when it tastes so good!" Then start eating as fast as you possibly can. Concentrate totally on your food and ignore your surroundings. The faster the better; don't be afraid to get messy!

5. Eating too greedily

Your job is to demonstrate eating greedily. Chow down the food in front of you. Even before you finish chewing, look around at the other food in the room. Act like there is not enough food in the world to satisfy your hunger and pleasure.

After you eat the food on your plate, jump out of your chair and grab the other food in the room. Stuff the food into your face—don't be afraid to send food flying and spilling down your front!